HERACLITUS

Translation and Analysis

Dennis Sweet

University Press of America,® Inc.
Lanham · Boulder · New York · Toronto · Plymouth, UK

Copyright © 1995 by
University Press of America,® Inc.
4501 Forbes Boulevard
Suite 200
Lanham, Maryland 20706
UPA Acquisitions Department (301) 459-3366

Estover Road
Plymouth PL6 7PY
United Kingdom

All rights reserved

British Library Cataloging in Publication Information Available

Library of Congress Cataloging-in-Publication Data

Heraclitus, of Ephesus.
[Fragments. English & Greek]
Heraclitus : translation and analysis / Dennis Sweet.
p. cm.
Includes bibliographical references and indexes.
1. Philosophy. 2. Heraclitus, of Ephesus.
3. Pre-Socratic philosophers. I. Sweet, Dennis.
B220.E5S94   1994   182'.4—dc20   94-17646 CIP

ISBN-13: 978-0-7618-3367-3 (pbk.)
ISBN-10: 0-7618-3367-6 (pbk.)

Contents

Preface	v
Acknowledgments	ix
Introduction	xi
Part One: Translation	1
Part Two: Analysis	55
Analysis of Themes	57
Index of Persons	73
Index of Terms	77
Bibliography	93

Preface

As with other Presocratic philosophers, all that remains of Heraclitus' published work is a fragmented group of quotations and paraphrases from later authors. Since we have no direct knowledge of how he arranged and organized his ideas, the order in which one presents the fragments is always a matter of conjecture.

Some translators have proceeded in terms of an interpretative approach, and have developed various *thematic arrangements* of the fragments based on recurring themes and words. Such thematic orchestrations (for example, the editions of Bywater [1877], Marcovich [1967], and Kahn [1979]) attempt to capture some of the coherence of Heraclitus' thought. Other translators have taken a more cautious approach, and have followed the *conventional arrangement* of the fragments that was instituted by Hermann Diels in his monumental *Die Fragmente der Vorsokratiker* (1901). Recognizing that any thematic arrangement of the fragments involves a good deal of speculation and interpretation on the part of the arranger, Diels presented them (more or less) according to the alphabetical order of the names of the sources from which the fragments were derived. This arrangement has, to a large extent, become the standard in Heraclitean scholarship. (See, for example, the editions of Bollack and Wismann [1972], and Freeman [1978].)

Each of these approaches to ordering the fragments has its strengths and its weaknesses. A strong point in favor of the first approach is that it provides a more coherent and unified view of Heraclitus' thought, and a deeper, more systematic appreciation of his views. This point, however, cuts both ways. For while it is generally assumed *that* there was some systematic order to Heraclitus' book, *how* it was expressed is a matter of speculation. A second, more pragmatic problem with the various thematic arrangements of the fragments is simply that they are inconsistent with the conventional arrangement, the one that is used in most of the scholarship. So, for example, to track down a standard reference to Diels' fragment 47, we must consult a concordance table, which tells us that fr. 47 is fr. 113 in Marcovich, and fr. XI in Kahn.

The primary strength of the conventional arrangement is that, for better or worse, it is the conventional arrangement. As I mentioned, part of Diels' reasoning behind arranging the fragments according to the alphabetical order of their sources was to avoid infecting them with his own interpretations, and to present them in a hermeneutically neutral fashion. The obvious downside of this approach is that when reading the fragments, one is confronted with a disjointed and incoherent muddle of ideas and images.

I have attempted to secure the advantage of each of these approaches by dividing the present work into two parts. Part One consists of a translation of all the fragments that are generally accepted in light of modern scholarship, presented in the conventional order instituted by Diels. In my translation I have tried to remain as faithful to the original Greek syntactical structures as modern English will allow, and to strike a medium between the overly literal and the excessively cosmetic styles characteristic of some earlier efforts. With respect to the more important words and idioms, I have generally employed the more archaic (and in certain cases, peculiarly Ionic) meanings over later ones.

Accompanying the translation is a running footnote commentary which provides information in three contexts. In the philological context, these notes serve to elucidate various problems of translation, and to provide the means for comparing my translation with others. In the semantic context, these footnotes provide some flexibility with regard to how one might interpret various words and phrases. Many of the terms that Heraclitus employs are intentionally ambiguous. And an understanding of the significance of a statement often depends upon an awareness the various meanings of the terms. Most translations fail to take into account these alternatives; thus they fail to convey the multiple layers of significance often expressed in the fragments. By calling attention to the variegated significance of certain words, I have tried to provide the reader with a means of uncovering some of these strange and wonderful layers of meaning. In the third, or general context, the footnotes serve to call attention to various stylistic points of interest; for example, the many puns, wordplays, neologisms, and stylistic innovations that Heraclitus employs. In this context the notes also serve to explain some of the obscure references and allusions found in the fragments.

While the translation in Part One proceeds in terms of the conventional arrangement of the fragments, the analyses in Part Two attempt to secure the advantages of a thematic arrangement. What makes Heraclitus both the most 'modern' and the most enigmatic writer of antiquity is that he often combines and weaves together several ideas or themes in a single statement. Thus, to understand Heraclitus the philosopher and to appreciate Heraclitus the literary innovator requires an understanding of his basic themes and how they are related to each other. Part Two begins with a systematic analysis of the basic philosophical themes expressed in Heraclitus' fragments. For each theme I provide a brief characterization and a list of the fragments expressing it. I have also indicated some of the inter-relationships among the themes by cross-referencing them. Following this is a brief description of each person Heraclitus refers to in the fragments. Part Two concludes with an index of all the important words contained in the fragments, and a bibliography of the works I have cited or consulted.

This translation of Heraclitus' fragments is based upon the fifth edition of Hermann Diels' *Die Fragmente der Vorsokratiker*, edited by Walther Kranz. In certain textually problematical areas (discussed in the footnotes) I have appealed to various emendations suggested by Marcovich, Bollack-Wismann, Kirk, Kahn, and others.

Words and phrases in parenthesis '( )' indicate probable glosses or paraphrases added by later sources. Words and phrases in brackets '[ ]' indicate my own paraphrasing, condensation, or restoration of an idea expressed in the context of the discussion surrounding the fragment. Boldface Roman numerals '**VI**' refer to the themes characterized in the first section of Part Two.

Acknowledgments

This book is largely the result of an undergraduate independent study project completed many years ago under the direction of Professor Paul D. Eisenberg, Department of Philosophy, Indiana University. I would like to express my gratitude to him for his help and guidance. I also wish to thank Michaela Weisstein, Michelle Godbout, J. Colin Sample, and Ling Yang for their assistance in transcribing and organizing the manuscript; and Dr. David Sider, Department of Classical Languages, Fordham University, who called my attention to various important paleographical points.

The Greek text was produced with the SSuperGreek TrueType font by Linguist's Software, P.O. Box 580, Edmonds, WA, 98020-0580.

Introduction

Heraclitus' Life

Little is known about Heraclitus. The chief source of information about the man and his work is Diogenes Laertius, who lived during the first half of the second century AD. In Book IX of his *Lives and Opinions of Eminent Philosophers*, Diogenes provides a brief biography of Heraclitus, which is composed of a few probable claims and several improbable anecdotes.

The claims that appear to be true are that Heraclitus, son of Bloson (or of Heracon), was born and lived in Ephesus (a Greek city on what is now the western coast of Turkey). He is described as a member of the aristocratic nobility (perhaps a descendant of Androclus, the founder of Ephesus), and is said to have given up his hereditary right of 'kingship' to his brother. According to the chronology of Apollodorus, Heraclitus reached his philosophical *acme* (which is traditionally regarded as the age of forty) in 504-501 BC, and probably died some twenty years later (around 480 BC).

What are generally regarded as the spurious aspects of Diogenes' biography are the less than flattering accounts of Heraclitus' personality and the events leading to his death; accounts which were, in all likelihood, created by less than sympathetic Hellenistic writers on the basis of views expressed in Heraclitus' work. In the following summary of Diogenes' narrative, I have inserted, in brackets, the numbers of the fragments on the basis of which the characteristic or event may have been concocted.

According to Diogenes, when Heraclitus reached maturity he claimed that he knew everything; not by virtue of any teacher, but rather by inquiring for himself [35, 40, 55, 57, 101, 129]. He took no part in the political life of his city, owing to his disdain of the populistic attitudes of his fellow citizens [121, 125a]. Instead he spent his time in the temple of Artemis playing dice games with the young boys [52].

Eventually Heraclitus' misanthropy compelled him to leave Ephesus and to live alone in the mountains, where he nourished himself with grasses and herbs. Because of his vegetarian diet [extrapolated from fr. 5?], Heraclitus fell victim to dropsy (the pathological accumulations of liquids in the body). He returned to Ephesus and visited the doctors, proposing to them this riddle: how do you make a drought after a heavy rain? Since the doctors were unable to understand, much less cure [58], Heraclitus' 'moist' condition [36, 76, 77, 126], he attempted to cure himself by going to a barn and burying himself in cow dung [96], presumably in the hope of drying the pathological moisture with the warmth of the manure [118]. This failed to have the desired effect, and Heraclitus died, at the age of sixty. (Diogenes notes an alternative ending, wherein Heraclitus was covered with dung and lay in the sun, in the hope of 'drying out'. After he died his dung-encrusted body was devoured by dogs, who failed to recognize the true nature of their meal [97].)

Heraclitus' Book

Diogenes Laertius tells us that Heraclitus wrote a single work, entitled *On Nature*, which was divided into three parts. The first part dealt with the universe, the second part with politics, and the third part was concerned with theology. According to Diogenes, Heraclitus made his work available by depositing it in the great temple of Artemis in Ephesus. Yet he intentionally composed the work in an obscure style so that only the most able and daring could grasp its meaning. Diogenes also refers to Theophrastus' assessment of the work as disjointed and unfinished, which the latter attributed to Heraclitus' 'impulsiveness'. (The word used by Theophrastus, *melagcholia*, has often been mistakenly interpreted in the more modern sense of 'melancholia', and has given support to the view of Heraclitus as the morose and sullen 'weeping philosopher'.)

These observations confirm what any reader of Heraclitus already knows: his writings are obscure. As with other Presocratic philosophers, we have only scattered, fragmented, and often cryptic remains of what was, presumably, a single, coherent treatise. What sets Heraclitus apart from these other writers, as evinced in the comments of Diogenes Laertius and Theophrastus, is that his work was originally scattered and fragmented, and intentionally obscure. Thus even among the ancient writers who had access to the entire book, Heraclitus was referred to as the 'riddler' (*ainiktes*) and the 'obscure one' (*skoteinos*).

The fact that Heraclitus was one of the first Greek prose writers might suggest that his enigmatic style was the result of the fact that the basic rules of prose writing had not yet been clearly established. While this is to some extent true, it does not mean that Heraclitus' obscurity was the result of his floundering about for the appropriate rules of lucid prose. Every indication, both in the fragments themselves and in the assessments of his ancient commentators, is that Heraclitus knew what he wanted to say and how he wanted to say it. Like a proto-Joyce, Heraclitus seems to have recognized the value of making his audience participate actively in the comprehension and appreciation of his work. Like the Delphic oracle, Heraclitus neither declares nor conceals, but shows by a sign.

Translation

1. τοῦ δὲ λόγου τοῦδ' ἐόντος ἀεὶ ἀξύνετοι γίνονται ἄνθρωποι καὶ πρόσθεν ἢ ἀκοῦσαι καὶ ἀκούσαντες τὸ πρῶτον· γινομένων γὰρ πάντων κατὰ τὸν λόγον τόνδε ἀπείροισιν ἐοίκασι, πειρώμενοι καὶ ἐπέων καὶ ἔργωντοιούτων, ὁκοίων ἐγὼ διηγεῦμαι κατὰ φύσιν διαιρέων ἕκαστον καὶ φράζων ὅκως ἔχει. τοὺς δὲ ἄλλους ἀνθρώπους λανθάνει ὁκόσα ἐγερθέντες ποιοῦσιν, ὅκωσπερ ὁκόσα εὕδοντες ἐπιλανθάνονται.

2. διὸ δεῖ ἕπεσθαι τῶι <ξυνῶι, τουτέστι τῶι> κοινῶι· ξυνὸς γὰρ ὁ κοινός. τοῦ λόγου δ' ἐόντος ξυνοῦ ζώουσιν οἱ πολλοὶ ὡς ἰδίαν ἔχοντες φρόνησιν.

1. (Sextus Empiricus, *Adversus mathematicos* VII 132.)

Of this eternally existing[1] *logos* people lack understanding, both before and after they hear the primary thing.[2] For since everything comes to be according to this *logos*, they are like ignorant people when experiencing such words[3] and actions as I expound—when I describe each according to its nature,[4] indicating how it is. But what other people do when awake is unnoticed [by them] just as they forget what they do when sleeping.

2. (*Ibid*., VII 133.)

Thus it is necessary[5] to follow[6] the common (that is, the universal: for 'common' is 'universal'). But although the *logos* is common, most people live as though they possess a private purpose.[7]

---

[1] I follow Diels and Zeller (after Clement, Hippolytus, and Amelius) in putting ἀεὶ with ἐόντος, *contra* Reinhardt, Snell, Gigon, and Kirk, who connect it with ἀξύνετοι. This seems to be a more natural grammatical construction and is more consistent with Heraclitus' doctrine of the eternity of the *logos*. Cf. fr. 30.

[2] Since τὸ πρῶτον contains an article and is in the accusative case, it is treated here as the object of ἀκοῦσαι and ἀκούσαντες. This interpretation implies the fundamental nature of the *logos* rather than simply indicating the first hearing of the idea (*contra* Kirk [1962], p. 33).

[3] *epeon* (ἐπέων)—also suggests oracular advice.

[4] *kata phusin* (κατὰ φύσιν) = according to its constitution.

[5] *dei* (δεῖ) suggests unconditional necessity. Cf. *chre* (χρή) in frs. 35, 43, 44, 80, and 114, which gives a more conditional sense of duty or obligation.

[6] *hepesthai* (ἕπεσθαι) also means 'to be obedient to'. Compare this word and its variant in fr. 1 (*epeon*) with the command of the Delphic oracle—*theo hepou* (θεῷ ἕπου) = obey God! The use of this particular word, coupled with the necessity implied at the beginning of the fragment, serves as a good example of what has been called Heraclitus' oracular style.

[7] *phronesis* (φρόνησις)—Alternative definitions of this word, such as 'to strive', 'to decide', and 'to intend', suggest "knowledge related to action." See Jaeger, p. 460.

3. (περὶ μεγέθους ἡλίου) εὖρος ποδὸς ἀνθρωπείου.

4. Si felicitas esset in delectationibus corporis, boves felices diceremus, cum inveniant orobum ad comedendum.

5. καθαίρονται δ' ἄλλωι αἵματι μιαινόμενοι οἷον εἴ τις εἰς πηλὸν ἐμβὰς πηλῶι ἀπονίζοιτο. μαίνεσθαι δ' ἂν δοκοίη, εἴ τις αὐτὸν ἀνθρώπων ἐπιφράσαιτο οὕτω ποιέοντα. καὶ τοῖς ἀγάλμασι δὲ τουτέοισιν εὔχονται, ὁκοῖον εἴ τις δόμοισι λεσχηνεύοιτο, οὔ τι γινώσκων θεοὺς οὐδ' ἥρωας οἵτινές εἰσι.

6. ὁ ἥλιος οὐ μόνον...νέος ἐφ' ἡμέρηι ἐστίν, ἀλλ' ἀεὶ νέος συνεχῶς.

7. εἰ πάντα τὰ ὄντα καπνὸς γένοιτο, ῥῖνες ἂν διαγνοῖεν.

8. τὸ ἀντίξουν συμφέρον καὶ ἐκ τῶν διαφερόντων καλλίστην ἁρμονίαν [καὶ πάντα κατ' ἔριν γίνεσθαι].

9. ὄνους σύρματ' ἂν ἑλέσθαι μᾶλλον ἢ χρυσόν....

3. (Aëtius, II 21.4.)
(Concerning the sun's size) the width of a human foot.[8]

4. (Albertus Magnus, *De vegetalibus* VI 401.)
If happiness was to be found in bodily pleasures, then we would say that cattle are happy when they find fodder to eat.

5. (Aristocritus, *Theosophia* 68. [Origen, *Contra Celsum* VII 62.])
They purify themselves vainly[9] by staining themselves with blood, just as a man, having stepped in dirt, may try to wash himself with dirt. He would appear crazy if any people were to observe him doing this. And they pray to these objects of worship, just as one might talk to houses, not knowing what gods and heroes really are.

6. (Aristotle, *Meteorologica* B. 2. 355a 13.)
The sun is (not only) new each day (but is always continually new).

7. (Aristotle, *De sensu* 5. 443a 23.)
If all existing things were to become smoke, then the nostrils would discern them.

8. (Aristotle, *Nicomachean Ethics* Θ 1. 1155b 4.)
What is in opposition is in agreement, and the most beautiful harmony comes out of things in conflict (and all happens[10] according to strife).

9. (*Ibid.*, K 5. 1176a 6.)
Donkeys would choose garbage over gold.

---

[8] In light of the recently discovered 'Derveni Papyrus' (fr. A), some scholars (e.g., Burkert [1983] and Sider [1987]) have suggested that this fragment and fr. 94 are parts of a single passage in Heraclitus' published work.

[9] *allos* (ἄλλως)—following Diels. Alternate meanings include 'without purpose' and 'without reason'.

[10] *ginesthai* (γίνεσθαι) = is born.

10. συνάψιες ὅλα καὶ οὐχ ὅλα, συμφερόμενον διαφερόμενον, συνᾶιδον διᾶιδον, καὶ ἐκ πάντων ἓν καὶ ἐξ ἑνὸς πάντα.

11. πᾶν γὰρ ἑρπετὸν πληγῆι νέμεται....

12. ποταμοῖσι τοῖσιν αὐτοῖσιν ἐμβαίνουσιν ἕτερα καὶ ἕτερα ὕδατα ἐπιρρεῖ·

13. a) δεῖ γὰρ τὸν χαρίεντα μήτε ῥυπᾶν μήτε αὐχμεῖν μήτε βορβόρωι χαίρειν....

b) ὕες βορβόρωι ἥδονται μᾶλλον ἢ καθαρῶι ὕδατι.

14. νυκτιπόλοις, μάγοις, βάκχοις, λήναις, μύσταις· τούτοις ἀπειλεῖ τὰ μετὰ θάνατον...τὰ γὰρ νομιζόμενα κατ' ἀνθρώπους μυστήρια ἀνιερωστὶ μυεῦνται.

10. (Aristotle, *De mundo* 5. 396b 20.)
Seizures[11]—wholes and non-wholes, being combined and differentiated, in accord and dissonant: unity is from everything and from everything is unity.

11. (*Ibid.*, 6. 401a 10.)
Every animal[12] is driven to pasture with a blow.

12. (Arius Didymus, ap. Eusebium P.E. XV 20.)
Upon those who step into the same stream ever different waters flow.

13. a) (Athen., V p. 178 f.)
(It is necessary that a real gentleman is neither dirty nor unwashed; nor should he [take] delight in mire.)

b) (Clement, *Stromateis* I 2.2.)
Pigs...take more pleasure in muck than in clean water.[13]

14. (Clement, *Protrepticus* 22.2.)
Nightroamers, wizards, Bacchants, revelers,[14] mystics (these [Heraclitus] threatened with death...) For the customs into which people are initiated are unholy mysteries.

---

[11] *sullapsies* (συλλάψιες)—following Marcovich, Kirk, etc., *contra* Diels' ουνάψιες. I have translated this word in its archaic sense, which gives the notion of physical seizure or grasping. Snell, Kirk, Marcovich, and Bollack-Wismann employ later senses ('Zusammensetzungen', 'things taken together', 'connections', and 'assemblages', respectively) in their translations. All of these terms suggest a putting together and unification of diverse things. Cf. the discussion of *harmonia* in **VIII**.

[12] *herpeton* (ἕρπετον)—In its later sense this means a four-footed beast. In its earlier, Homeric sense it was used by the gods when referring to humans.

[13] Cf. fr. 37.

[14] *lenais* (λήναις)—translated literally by Patrick and Bywater (fragment 124) as Lenai. It denotes the celebrants of the Lenaea, an Athenian festival of wine and contests held in January-February in honor of Bacchus. See Nilsson, p. 275 ff.

15. εἰ μὴ γὰρ Διονύσωι πομπὴν ἐποιοῦντο καὶ ὕμνεον ἆισμα αἰδοίοισιν, ἀναιδέστατα εἴργαστ' ἄν· ὡυτὸς δὲ Ἀΐδης καὶ Διόνυσος, ὅτεωι μαίνονται καὶ ληναΐζουσιν.

16. τὸ μὴ δῦνόν ποτε πῶς ἄν τις λάθοι;

17. οὐ γὰρ φρονέουσι τοιαῦτα πολλοί, ὁκόσοι ἐγκυρεῦσιν, οὐδὲ μαθόντες γινώσκουσιν, ἑωυτοῖσι δὲ δοκέουσι.

18. ἐὰν μὴ ἔλπηται, ἀνέλπιστον οὐκ ἐξευρήσει, ἀνεξερεύνητον ἐὸν καὶ ἄπορον.

19. ἀκοῦσαι οὐκ ἐπιστάμενοι οὐδ' εἰπεῖν.

15. (*Ibid.*, 34.5.)

If it were not in honor of Dionysos that they organize a procession and sing the phallic[15] hymn, what they do would be most shameless: but Hades and Dionysos are one and the same, in whose honor people rave and celebrate the Bacchic revelry.

16. (Clement, *Paedagogus* II 99.5.)

How could anyone be unobserved by that which never sets?

17. (Clement, *Stromateis* II 8.1.)

Most people do not comprehend[16] however they encounter such things, nor do they understand what they learn; they believe only themselves.

18. (*Ibid.*, II 17.4.)

If one doesn't hope one will not find the unhoped for—it is inscrutable and impracticable.

19. (*Ibid.*, 24.5.)

They know neither how to listen nor how to speak.

---

[15] Since the word used here is *aidoioisin* (αἰδοίοισιν) rather than the contextually more accurate *phallikos* (φαλλικός), Heraclitus clearly intends a wordplay between *aidoion* (αἰδοῖον) = the genitals; *aidoios* (αἰδοῖος) = august, venerable; *anaidestata* (ἀναιδέστατα) = most shameless; and *Aides* (Ἀΐδης) = Hades. The first three of these words share a common etymological origin, which is expressed in the verb *aideomai* (αἰδέομαι). This word combines the feelings of shame and fear with the notions of awe, reverence, and respect. The apparently distinct ideas expressed by these different words, which are combined by virtue of a common origin, lends to the overall effect of the fragment: the combination of the notions of life (Dionysos) and death (Hades) into a union that is more fundamental than its individual constituent parts.

[16] *ou gar phroneousi* (οὐ γὰρ φρονέουσι)—see footnote 7.

20. γενόμενοι ζώειν ἐθέλουσι μόρους τ' ἔχειν, μᾶλλον δὲ ἀναπαύεσθαι, καὶ παῖδας καταλείπουσι μόρους γενέσθαι.

21. θάνατός ἐστιν ὁκόσα ἐγερθέντες ὁρέομεν, ὁκόσα δὲ εὕδοντες ὕπνος.

22. χρυσὸν γὰρ οἱ διζήμενοι γῆν πολλὴν ὀρύσσουσι καὶ εὑρίσκουσιν ὀλίγον.

23. Δίκης ὄνομα οὐκ ἂν ἤιδεσαν, εἰ ταῦτα μὴ ἦν.

24. ἀρηιφάτους θεοὶ τιμῶσι καὶ ἄνθρωποι.

20. (*Ibid.*, III 14.1.)
Being born they want to live to have their appointed fates[17] (yet more than this they want repose[18])—and they leave children behind to have their fates happen to them.[19]

21. (*Ibid.*, III 21.1.)
Death is what we see when awake, but what we see when sleeping is sleep.

22. (*Ibid.*, IV 4.2.)
Those seeking gold dig much earth and discover little.

23. (*Ibid.*, IV 9.7.)
They would not have known the name of Justice[20] if these things did not exist.[21]

24. (*Ibid.*, IV 16.1.)
Gods and men honor those slain in battle.

---

[17] *morous* (μόρους) = dooms, deaths, destinies.

[18] *anapauesthai* (ἀναπαύεσθαι)—The idea here is sleep with the purpose of regaining one's strength. This line may be a later addition.

[19] This fragment begins and ends with similar words (*genomenoi* = being born; and *genesthai* = to happen). Such repetition of the same or a similar term as the first and last words of a fragment illustrates Heraclitus' so-called 'ring construction'. Similar constructions are found in frs. 10, 36, 62, 79 and 88.

[20] *Dike* (Δίκη) = enlightened justice, personified as the daughter of Zeus (power) and Themis (law). See Hesiod, *Theogony* 901 ff.

[21] Since the subject referred to as "these things" is not given, the meaning of this fragment is unclear. Clement, who is the source of the quotation, suggests that 'the laws' is the subject. This, however, is hard to defend in light of the entire quotation. Given Heraclitus' penchant for representing justice in a concrete way (as in frs. 28b and 94), and in light of his doctrine of the unity of opposites (see VII), "these things" might refer to concrete instances of injustice, whose existence is understood to be reciprocally dependent upon concrete instances of justice. See the discussion of this problem in Kirk [1962], pp. 125-29.

25. μόροι γὰρ μέζονες μέζονας μοίρας λαγχάνουσι.

26. ἄνθρωπος ἐν εὐφρόνηι φάος ἅπτεται ἑαυτῶι [ἀποθανὼν] ἀποσβεσθεὶς ὄψεις, ζῶν δὲ ἅπτεται τεθνεῶτος εὕδων, [ἀποσβεσθεὶς ὄψεις], ἐγρηγορὼς ἅπτεται εὕδοντος.

27. ἀνθρώπους μένει ἀποθανόντας ἄσσα οὐκ ἔλπονται οὐδὲ δοκέουσιν.

25. *(Ibid.*, IV 49.2.)
Greater destinies obtain greater rewards.[22]

26. *(Ibid.*, IV 141.2.)
A man lightens[23] himself in the night[24] when he is extinguished (as is his vision). Living, he joins[25] with the dead while he sleeps; waking, he joins with one sleeping.

27. *(Ibid.*, IV 144.3.)
What awaits people in death they neither anticipate[26] nor even imagine.[27]

---

[22] There is a wordplay here upon the cognates *moroi* (μόροι) = destinies, and *moiras* (μοῖρας) = shares. The latter, though, takes on the particular meaning of 'divine rewards', or 'gifts of fate' when coupled, as it is here, with the verb *lagchano* (λαγχάνω).

[23] The recurring verb in this enigmatic fragment is *haptetai* (ἅπτεται), which has generally been translated as 'kindles'. (Cf. Diels, Freeman, Burnet, Kirk and Raven, etc.) This, however, gives an active sense to a middle/passive voice. It also fails to convey another important notion inherent in the fragment, the notion of immortality. By translating this verb as 'lightens', I have tried to preserve the idea of 'kindling' in a more middle/passive sense, while also suggesting the idea of the soul's being 'lightened' of the burden of the physical body at the time of death. This second interpretation is further suggested by the phrase ἀποθανὼν ἀποσβεσθεὶς ὄψεις = the man is extinguished with respect to his vision. Of all the commentators on this fragment, Kahn ([1979], p. 214) is the only one to suggest this line of interpretation, although he does not give any indication of it in his translation.

[24] *en euphrone* (ἐν εὐφρόνῃ)—since Heraclitus uses this euphemism for night (which literally means 'the pleasant time') rather than the more literal *nox* (νύξ), Stöhr has suggested that the notion of death is implied (see the previous note). (Cf. Stöhr, pp. 20, 50, 52; and Cleve, pp. 73-76.) The curious dual meaning of this fragment seems to suggest a day/night, waking/sleeping, life/death correspondence.

[25] Here, and again later in the fragment, *haptetai* is translated as 'joins'. The idea is that of fastening oneself to something, or grasping.

[26] *elpontai* (ἔλπονται) = hope for.

[27] *dokeousi* (δοκέουσι) = believe, suppose, guess.

28. a) δοκέοντα γὰρ ὁ δοκιμώτατος γινώσκει, φυλάσσει·

b) καὶ μέντοι καὶ Δίκη καταλήψεται ψευδῶν τέκτονας καὶ μάρτυρας.

29. αἱρεῦνται γὰρ ἓν ἀντὶ ἁπάντων οἱ ἄριστοι, κλέος ἀέναον θνητῶν· οἱ δὲ πολλοὶ κεκόρηνται ὅκωσπερ κτήνεα.

30. κόσμον τόνδε, τὸν αὐτὸν ἁπάντων, οὔτε τις θεῶν οὔτε ἀνθρώπων ἐποίησεν, ἀλλ' ἦν ἀεὶ καὶ ἔστιν καὶ ἔσται πῦρ ἀείζωον, ἁπτόμενον μέτρα καὶ ἀποσβεννύμενον μέτρα.

31. a) πυρὸς τροπαὶ πρῶτον θάλασσα, θαλάσσης δὲ τὸ μὲν ἥμισυ γῆ, τὸ δὲ ἥμισυ πρηστήρ.

b) <γῆ> θάλασσα διαχέεται, καὶ μετρέεται εἰς τὸν αὐτὸν λόγον, ὁκοῖος πρόσθεν ἦν ἢ γενέσθαι γῆ.

28. (Ibid., V 9.3.)

a) The most esteemed man knows only imaginings,[28] which he guards.

b) Justice will seize the fabricators of lies and those who testify to them.

29. (Ibid., V 59.4.)

The most noble people choose one thing against all else: ever-flowing glory among mortals. Most people, though, have sated themselves like sheep.

30. (Ibid., V 103.6.)

The order,[29] the same for all, was made neither by gods nor by humans, but it was always and is and will be fire ever-living—being lighted[30] in measures and going out in measures.

31. (Ibid., V 104.3-5.)

a) Alterations[31] of fire: first sea, but of sea half is earth, half is lightning-storm.

b) (Earth) is dispersed into sea and is measured in the same *logos*[32] as it was before it became earth.

---

[28] Here there is a play upon the words *ho dokimotatos* (ὁ δοκιμώτατος) = the most esteemed man, and *dokeonta* (δοκέοντα) = imaginings.

[29] *kosmos* (κόσμος)—I have chosen the archaic meaning of this word rather than the later, 'cosmic' sense employed by Plato. In Homer the word is used to denote a pleasing form, an ornament, or decoration.

[30] For *aptomenon* (ἁπτόμενον) and *aposbennumenon* (ἀποσβεννύμενον), see footnote 23.

[31] *tropai* (τρόπαι) = reversal, turning around. This word also suggests a temporal sequence; for example, the reversal of the sun at the solstices.

[32] *logos* (λόγος) = proportion, amount. Cf. fr. 90.

32. ἓν τὸ σοφὸν μοῦνον λέγεσθαι οὐκ ἐθέλει καὶ ἐθέλει Ζηνὸς ὄνομα.

33. νόμος καὶ βουλῆι πείθεσθαι ἑνός.

34. ἀξύνετοι ἀκούσαντες κωφοῖσιν ἐοίκασι· φάτις αὐτοῖσιν μαρτυρεῖ παρεόντας ἀπεῖναι.

35. χρὴ γὰρ εὖ μάλα πολλῶν ἵστορας φιλοσόφους ἄνδρας εἶναι....

36. ψυχῆισιν θάνατος ὕδωρ γενέσθαι, ὕδατι δὲ θάνατος γῆν γενέσθαι, ἐκ γῆς δὲ ὕδωρ γίνεται, ἐξ ὕδατος δὲ ψυχή.

37. Si modo credimus Ephesio Heracleto qui ait sues caeno, cohortales aves pulvere vel cinere lavari.

38. [Sc. Thales] δοκεῖ δὲ κατά τινας πρῶτος ἀστρολογῆσαι... μαρτυρεῖ δ᾽ αὐτῶι καὶ ʽΗ. καὶ Δημόκριτος.

32. (*Ibid.*, V 115.1.)
The wise is one, alone—unwilling and willing to be spoken of by the name Zeus.[33]

33. (*Ibid.*, V 115.2.)
It is law to obey the will[34] of one.

34. (*Ibid.*, V 115.3.)
Those listening without understanding are like the deaf. The saying bears witness to them: absent while being present.

35. (*Ibid.*, V 140.5.)
The person who loves wisdom must be a good inquirer into a great many things.

36. (*Ibid.*, VI 17.2.)
For souls it is death to become water; for water it is death to become earth: out of earth comes water; out of water, soul.

37. (Columella, VIII 4.4.)
Pigs take more pleasure in mire than in clean water;[35] chickens bathe in dust.

38. (Diogenes Laertius, *Vitæ* I 23.)
(Thales practiced astronomy.)[36]

---

[33] *Zenos* (Ζηνός)—a poetic variant of 'Zeus', which reflects a close etymological relationship with *zao* (ζάω) = to live.

[34] *boule* (βουλῇ) = counsel, design, intention.

[35] Cf. fr. 13b.

[36] Cf. fr. 105, where the same claim is made about Homer.
In Heraclitus' time the word *astrologia* (ἀστρολογία) was used to refer to both astronomy and astrology, inasmuch as these practices had not yet been clearly distinguished. See Lloyd, pp. 177 ff.

39. ἐν Πριήνηι Βίας ἐγένετο ὁ Τευτάμεω, οὗ πλείων λόγος ἢ τῶν ἄλλων.

40. πολυμαθίη νόον ἔχειν οὐ διδάσκει· Ἡσίοδον γὰρ ἂν ἐδίδαξε καὶ Πυθαγόρην αὖτίς τε Ξενοφάνεά τε καὶ Ἑκαταῖον.

41. εἶναι γὰρ ἓν τὸ σοφόν, ἐπίστασθαι γνώμην, ὁτέη ἐκυβέρνησε πάντα διὰ πάντων.

42. τόν τε Ὅμηρον ἔφασκεν ἄξιον ἐκ τῶν ἀγώνων ἐκβάλλεσθαι καὶ ῥαπίζεσθαι καὶ Ἀρχίλοχον ὁμοίως.

43. ὕβριν χρὴ σβεννύναι μᾶλλον ἢ πυρκαϊήν.

44. μάχεσθαι χρὴ τὸν δῆμον ὑπὲρ τοῦ νόμου ὅκωσπερ τείχεος.

39. *(Ibid.,* I 88.)
In Priene was born Bias, son of Teutames, who is more esteemed[37] than other men.

40. *(Ibid.,* IX 1.)
Learning many things[38] does not teach good sense;[39] for it would have taught Hesiod and Pythagoras, and also Xenophanes and Hecataeus.

41. *(Ibid.,* IX 1.)
The wise is one: to understand the purpose[40] by which it steers everything through all.

42. *(Ibid.,* IX 1.)
Indeed Homer deserves to be cast out of the contests and beaten with the staff,[41] and Archilochus, too.

43. *(Ibid.,* IX 2.)
One ought to quench insolence more than a flaring fire.

44. *(Ibid.,* IX 2.)
The people must fight for the law just as for the city wall.[42]

---

[37] *logos* (λόγος)—this usage suggests high regard and reputation.

[38] *polymathie* (πολυμαθίη)—a cognate with *mathontes* (fr. 17) and *mathesis* (fr. 55) = learning. This term (i.e., polymath) was probably coined by Heraclitus.

[39] *noon* (νόον) = mindfulness, understanding. Cf. frs. 104, 114.

[40] *gnomen* (γνώμην) = insight, recognition, judgment, plan. Cf. fr. 78.

[41] *hrapizesthai* (ῥαπίζεσθαι)—from *hrabdos* (ῥάβδος), the staff held by the rhapsode, or professional bard, during public competitions. The meaning of this fragment appears to be that Homer and Archilochus should be punished by means of their own poetic arts.

The idea of 'poetic punishment' might refer to a legend associated with Archilochus. When Lycambes first promised and then refused his daughter's hand in marriage to Archilochus, the enraged poet composed an iambic lampoon against the man's family of such power that all of Lycambes' daughters hanged themselves in shame.

[42] Cf. fr. 114.

45. ψυχῆς πείρατα ἰὼν οὐκ ἂν ἐξεύροιο, πᾶσαν ἐπιπορευόμενος ὁδόν· οὕτω βαθὺν λόγον ἔχει.

46. τήν τε οἴησιν ἱερὰν νόσον ἔλεγε καὶ τὴν ὅρασιν ψεύδεσθαι.

47. μὴ εἰκῆ περὶ τῶν μεγίστων συμβαλλώμεθα.

48. βίος· τῶι οὖν τόξωι ὄνομα βίος, ἔργον δὲ θάνατος.

49. εἷς ἐμοὶ μύριοι, ἐὰν ἄριστος ἦι.

a) ποταμοῖς τοῖς αὐτοῖς ἐμβαίνομέν τε καὶ οὐκ ἐμβαίνομεν, εἶμέν τε καὶ οὐκ εἶμεν.

50. οὐκ ἐμοῦ, ἀλλὰ τοῦ λόγου ἀκούσαντας ὁμολογεῖν σοφόν ἐστιν ἓν πάντα εἶναι....

45. *(Ibid., IX 7.)*
You will not discover the limits of the soul by wandering, even if you travel every way—so deep is its *logos*.[43]

46. *(Ibid., IX 7.)*
(Self-conceit: a sacred disease [i.e., epilepsy]; and to see is to be deceived.)[44]

47. *(Ibid., IX 73.)*
Let us not randomly reckon about the greatest matters.

48. *(Etymologicum magnum; s.v.* βίος.)
The bow's name is life,[45] its deed is death.

49. (Theodorus Prodromus, *Epistulae* 1. Galen, *De diff. puls.* VIII 773K, inserts ἐμοί at the beginning.)
(For me) one person is [worth] ten thousand, if that person is the best.

a) In the same streams we both step and do not step; we both are and are not.

50. (Hippolytus, *Refutatio* IX 9.1.)
Listening not to me but rather to the *logos* it is wise to agree[46] that all things are one.

---

[43] *logos* = measure, law.

[44] A dubious quotation. Cf. fr. 107.

[45] A play upon the words *biós* (βιός = an archaic word for a bow) and *bíos* (βίος = life). The difference in the written accentuation was unknown in Heraclitus' day.

[46] A play upon the words *logos* and *homologein* = to agree.

51. οὐ ξυνιᾶσιν ὅκως διαφερόμενον ἑωυτῶι ὁμολογέει· παλίντροπος ἁρμονίη ὅκωσπερ τόξου καὶ λύρης.

52. αἰὼν παῖς ἐστι παίζων, πεσσεύων· παιδὸς ἡ βασιληίη.

53. Πόλεμος πάντων μὲν πατήρ ἐστι, πάντων δὲ βασιλεύς, καὶ τοὺς μὲν θεοὺς ἔδειξε τοὺς δὲ ἀνθρώπους, τοὺς μὲν δούλους ἐποίησε τοὺς δὲ ἐλευθέρους.

54. ἁρμονίη ἀφανὴς φανερῆς κρείττων.

51. (Ibid., IX 9.2.)

They do not comprehend how being at variance[47] it agrees[48] with itself: it is a harmony[49] turning back upon itself[50] like a bow and a lyre.

52. (Ibid., IX 9.4.)

Life[51] is a child playing, moving the pieces in a game:[52] kingship belongs to the child.

53. (Ibid., IX 9.4.)

War is the father of all, the king of all, and he has shown some as gods, others as humans; he has made some slaves, others free.

54. (Ibid., IX 9.5.)

The hidden harmony is superior[53] to the visible.

---

[47] *diapheromenon* (διαφερόμενον) = quarreling, differing from.

[48] I follow Diels and Kahn in using the unaltered text of Hippolytus. Here we read *homologeei* (ὁμολογέει) = it agrees, *contra* Zeller's, Marcovich's, and Kirk's less plausible substitution of *xumpheretai* (ξυμφέρεται) = it is gathered.

[49] *harmonie* (ἁρμονίη) = fitting together. This word is used figuratively by Homer (*Iliad*, XXII 225) to mean an agreement between hostile parties. It is also used by Hesiod (*Theogony*, 937) to personify reconciliation, the child of Aphrodite (love) and Ares (conflict). Cf. **VIII**.

[50] *palintropos* (παλίντροπος) resembles *palintonos* (παλίντονος), an epithet used by Homer to describe a bow.

[51] My interpretation of the 'timely' problem concerning how to translate *aion* (αἰών) should be understood in two ways: first, in the sense employed by Homer to refer to a human lifetime; and second, in the more abstract sense of all life, that is, the life of the world. Compare the similar senses expressed in the Latin *vita*.

[52] *pessoi* (πεσσοί)—The game indicated by this word suggests both order (rules of play) and, at least in this context, chance. Regardless of whether dice were used, chance is certainly a factor in view of the child's whim to follow the rules or to ignore them. The coexistence of chance and order, though paradoxical, may be intended to suggest a higher order which remains unknown to most people. For a brief discussion of this, see **IX** and **XVIII**.

[53] *kreitton* (κρείττων) = stronger, more desirable. See **VIII**.

55. ὅσων ὄψις ἀκοὴ μάθησις, ταῦτα ἐγὼ προτιμέω.

56. ἐξηπάτηνται...οἱ ἄνθρωποι πρὸς τὴν γνῶσιν τῶν φανερῶν παραπλησίως Ὁμήρωι, ὃς ἐγένετο τῶν Ἑλλήνων σοφώτερος πάντων. ἐκεῖνόν τε γὰρ παῖδες φθεῖρας κατακτείνοντες ἐξηπάτησαν εἰπόντες· ὅσα εἴδομεν καὶ ἐλάβομεν, ταῦτα ἀπολείπομεν, ὅσα δὲ οὔτε εἴδομεν οὔτ' ἐλάβομεν, ταῦτα φέρομεν.

57. διδάσκαλος δὲ πλείστων Ἡσίοδος· τοῦτον ἐπίστανται πλεῖστα εἰδέναι, ὅστις ἡμέρην καὶ εὐφρόνην οὐκ ἐγίνωσκεν· ἔστι γὰρ ἕν.

58. οἱ γοῦν ἰατροί...τέμνοντες, καίοντες, πάντηι βασανίζοντες κακῶς τοὺς ἀρρωστοῦντας, ἐπαιτέονται μηδὲν ἄξιοι μισθὸν λαμβάνειν παρὰ τῶν ἀρρωστούντων, ταὐτὰ ἐργαζόμενοι, τὰ ἀγαθὰ καὶ τὰς νόσους.

55. (*Ibid.*, IX 9.5.)
Whatever comes from sight, hearing, learning by inquiry—these things I honor.[54]

56. (*Ibid.*, IX 9.5.)
People are thoroughly beguiled regarding the knowledge of manifest things, as was Homer, who was wisest of all the Greeks. For he was beguiled[55] by boys killing lice, who said: 'what we saw and seized, those we leave behind; what we neither saw nor seized, those we bring'.

57. (*Ibid.*, IX 10.2.)
The teacher of most people is Hesiod. They understand him to be the most knowing; he who failed to recognize day and night,[56] for they are one.

58. (*Ibid.*, IX 10.3.)
Doctors who cut and burn (and evilly torture the sick in every way) complain that the fees they receive are unworthy of their doing these things (the cure having the same effect as the disease).[57]

---

[54] *protimeo* (προτιμέω) = prefer, esteem.

[55] *exepatentai* (ἐξηπάτηνται)—This word has generally been translated as 'deceived'. However, 'beguiled' seems to be a closer translation within the context of the fragment. What is described here is the traditional story of how blind Homer was unable to guess the boys' riddle, and so died of chagrin.

[56] A reference to Hesiod's *Theogony*, 743-54, where Day and Night are personified and described as going in opposite directions.

[57] The latter part of this fragment (enclosed in parenthesis) is probably a later gloss. See Kirk [1962], pp. 92-96.

59. γναφείωι ὁδὸς εὐθεῖα καὶ σκολιὴ (ἡ τοῦ ὀργάνου τοῦ καλουμένου κοχλίου ἐν τῶι γναφείωι περιστροφὴ εὐθεῖα καὶ σκολιή· ἄνω γὰρ ὁμοῦ καὶ κύκλωι περιέρχεται) μία ἐστί...καὶ ἡ αὐτή.

60. ὁδὸς ἄνω κάτω μία καὶ ὠυτή.

61. θάλασσα ὕδωρ καθαρώτατον καὶ μιαρώτατον, ἰχθύσι μὲν πότιμον καὶ σωτήριον, ἀνθρώποις δὲ ἄποτον καὶ ὀλέθριον.

62. ἀθάνατοι θνητοί, θνητοὶ ἀθάνατοι, ζῶντες τὸν ἐκείνων θάνατον, τὸν δὲ ἐκείνων βίον τεθνεῶτες.

63. ἔνθα δ' ἐόντι ἐπανίστασθαι καὶ φύλακας γίνεσθαι ἐγερτὶ ζώντων καὶ νεκρῶν.

59. (*Ibid*., IX 10.4.)

Of letters [or, of writers] the way is straight and crooked (the working of what is called the *kochlias*,[58] spinning around in the carding-comb,[59] is straight and crooked, for it goes both upward and around, it goes round and returns); it is one and the same.

60. (*Ibid*., IX 10.4.)

The way up and down is one and the same.

61. (*Ibid*., IX 10.5.)

Sea is the most pure and most polluted water. For fish it is drinkable and life-preserving; for people it is undrinkable and deadly.

62. (*Ibid*., IX 10.6.)

Immortals are mortal, mortals are immortal; living the other's death, being dead in the other's life.

63. (*Ibid*., IX 10.6.)

...to be raised[60] and to become active[61] guardians[62] of those living and dead.

---

[58] This word literally denotes a snail with a spiral shell, and is taken by Kirk ([1962], p. 98 fn.) to refer to a mechanical screw.

[59] *gnapheio* (γναφείῳ)—I treat this word as a cognate of *knaphos* (κνάφος) = 'carding-comb'. This suggests the idea of the movable teeth of the carding-comb, which rotate in the direction of the comb's stroke.

[60] The text here is extremely corrupt. The beginning word that Hippolytus gives seems to be alluding to the resurrection of the body after death. However, the verb *epanistasthai* (ἐπανίστασθαι) seems improper in this context, since in Herodotus it is used to indicate a political uprising. Perhaps, then, the prefix ἐπ- is later corruption; for its elimination gives us *anistasthai* (ἀνίστασθαι), which provides the proper sense of a posthumous 'rising up'.

[61] *egerti* (ἐγερτί) = busy, eager, wakeful.

[62] This is an allusion to Hesiod's *Works and Days* (110 ff.), where the people who lived during the Golden Age are described as having become spirits that keep watch over mortals. Hesiod also refers, in line 116, to the identification of Death with Sleep—an idea explicit in Homer (e.g. *Iliad*, XIV 231) and implicit in Heraclitus (see **XII**).

64. τὰ δὲ πάντα οἰακίζει Κεραυνός....

65. ...χρησμοσύνην καὶ κόρον·

66. πάντα γάρ...τὸ πῦρ ἐπελθὸν κρινεῖ καὶ καταλήψεται.

67. ὁ θεὸς ἡμέρη εὐφρόνη, χειμὼν θέρος, πόλεμος εἰρήνη, κόρος λιμός (τἀναντία ἅπαντα· οὗτος ὁ νοῦς), ἀλλοιοῦται δὲ ὅκωσπερ <πῦρ> ὁπόταν συμμιγῆι θυώμασιν, ὀνομάζεται καθ' ἡδονὴν ἑκάστου.

68. καὶ διὰ τοῦτο εἰκότως αὐτὰ ἄκεα ʽΗ. προσεῖπεν ὡς ἐξακεσόμενα τὰ δεινὰ καὶ τὰς ψυχὰς ἐξάντεις ἀπεργαζόμενα τῶν ἐν τῆι γενέσει συμφορῶν.

64. (*Ibid.*, IX 10.7.)
A thunderbolt[63] steers[64] all these things.

65. (*Ibid.*, IX 10.7.)
[Regarding fire]: need[65] and surfeit.

66. (*Ibid.*, IX 10.7.)
Fire, having come upon them, will distinguish[66] and seize all things.

67. (*Ibid.*, IX 10.8.)
The God: day/night, winter/summer, war/peace, satiety/hunger.[67] [He][68] is changed in the manner (of fire) when it is mingled with spices and is named according to the delight of each of them.

68. (Iamblichus, *De mysteriis* I 11.)
[Heraclitus called the perceptions of shameful things as holy] 'remedies'.[69]

---

[63] This was the weapon used by Zeus to control the world. Hippolytus identifies it with Heraclitus' notion of fire.

[64] *oiakizei* (οἰακίζει) = guides, manages.

[65] *chresmosune* (χρησμοσύνη) = want, poverty, importunity.

[66] *krinei* (κρίνει) = separate, pick out, choose, decide, judge.

[67] These four pairs of antithetical nouns are presented without copulas or syntactical reference, so the first word ('the God') is regarded as the subject. Similar antithetical constructions are expressed in frs. 10, 48, 57, 59, 60, 65, 76, 82, 84a, 88, 111, and 126.

[68] 'He' (God, or *logos*) is the implied subject given at the beginning of the fragment.

[69] *akea* (ἀκέα) = cures, repairs. Iamblichus here compares Heraclitus' idea concerning the effects of perceiving shameful things as holy (cf. fr. 15) to Aristotle's notion of the cathartic effects of tragedy upon the emotions of the viewer. See **XV**.

69. θυσιῶν τοίνυν τίθημι διττὰ εἴδη· τὰ μὲν τῶν ἀποκεκαθαρμένων παντάπασιν ἀνθρώπων, οἷα ἐφ' ἑνὸς ἄν ποτε γένοιτο σπανίως...ἤ τινων ὀλίγων εὐαριθμήτων ἀνδρῶν· τὰ δ' ἔνυλα κτλ.

70. παίδων ἀθύρματα νενόμικεν εἶναι τὰ ἀνθρώπινα δοξάσματα.

71. μεμνῆσθαι δὲ καὶ τοῦ ἐπιλανθανομένου ἧι ἡ ὁδὸς ἄγει.

72. ὧι μάλιστα διηνεκῶς ὁμιλοῦσι λόγωι τῶι τὰ ὅλα διοικοῦντι, τούτωι διαφέρονται, καὶ οἷς καθ' ἡμέραν ἐγκυροῦσι, ταῦτα αὐτοῖς ξένα φαίνεται.

73. οὐ δεῖ ὥσπερ καθεύδοντας ποιεῖν καὶ λέγειν· καὶ γὰρ καὶ τότε δοκοῦμεν ποιεῖν καὶ λέγειν.

74. οὐ δεῖ <ὡς> παῖδας τοκεώνων, τοῦτ' ἔστι κατὰ ψιλόν· καθότι παρειλήφαμεν.

75. τοὺς καθεύδοντας οἶμαι...ἐργάτας εἶναι λέγει καὶ συνεργοὺς τῶν ἐν τῶι κόσμωι γινομένων.

69. *(Ibid.*, V 15.)
(There are two kinds of sacrifice. One kind is made by wholly purified people, such as rarely occurs in an individual, or only in a very few. The other kind is material and corporeal.)[70]

70. (Iamblichus, *De anima*. [Stobaeus II 1.16.])
(Human opinions are children's playthings.)[71]

71. (Marcus Aurelius, IV 46.)
(One must also remember the person who forgets where the way leads.)

72. *(Ibid.*, IV 46.)
(They are at variance with that which they most continuously associate, and what they meet with by day appears strange to them.)

73. *(Ibid.*, IV 46.)
(We should not act or speak like sleeping people.)

74. *(Ibid.*, IV 46.)
(We should not [act or speak] like our parent's children, in the manner we received.)

75. *(Ibid.*, VI 42.)
(Those sleeping are laborers and coworkers with the things happening in the world.)[72]

---

[70] Both here and in the next fragment Iamblichus is paraphrasing Heraclitus.

[71] *athurmata* (ἀθύρματα) = toys, delights, joys. See **X (B), XI (B)**.

[72] *toi kosmoi* (τῶι κόσμωι) = the order. See **IX**.

76. πυρὸς θάνατος ἀέρι γένεσις, καὶ ἀέρος θάνατος ὕδατι γένεσις.

77. ψυχῆισι φάναι τέρψιν ἢ θάνατον ὑγρῆισι γενέσθαι.

78. ἦθος γὰρ ἀνθρώπειον μὲν οὐκ ἔχει γνώμας, θεῖον δὲ ἔχει.

79. ἀνὴρ νήπιος ἤκουσε πρὸς δαίμονος ὅκωσπερ παῖς πρὸς ἀνδρός.

76. (Plutarch, *De E apud Delphous* 392 C.)
(The death of fire is the birth of air, and the death of air is the birth of water.)[73]

77. (Porphyry, *De antro Nympharum* 10. [Numenius fr. 30 = Theodinga fr. 35.])
It is delight or[74] death for souls to become moist.

78. (Origen, *Contra Celsum* VI 12.)
Human character has no purpose;[75] the divine, however, has.

79. (*Ibid.*, VI 12.)
Man has heard himself called childish[76] by a god, just as a child has by a man.

---

[73] I follow Kahn in quoting Plutarch rather than the more commonly quoted (e.g., Diels, Bywater) version given by Maximus of Tyre (XII 4.), since Plutarch is a more reliable source with regard to Heraclitus.

[74] I follow Diels and Marcovich in reading ἤ (*contra* Kahn's μή), since it lends itself more readily to the two senses of a 'moist soul' which Heraclitus intends. On the one hand, a moist soul is said to be found in the person who is drunk or ignorant (confused by appearances). On the other hand, when the ignorant person dies, that person's moist soul disintegrates and unites with water in an endless cycle of elemental change. See **XIV**.

[75] *gnomas* (γνώμας) = will, intention. Cf. fr. 41.

[76] *aner nepios ekouse* (ἀνὴρ νήπιος ἤκουσε)—This phrase idiomatically means 'a man is considered childish'. I have chosen a more literal translation in order to stress the recurring Heraclitean themes of hearing and speaking (see **XVI** and **II**, respectively). The latter notion is implied here by the word *nepios*, which idiomatically means 'silly' and 'childlike', while literally it means 'not yet speaking'. For further indications of this theme, see frs. 1, 19, 34, and 50.

80. εἰδέναι δὲ χρὴ τὸν πόλεμον ἐόντα ξυνόν, καὶ δίκην ἔριν, καὶ γινόμενα πάντα κατ' ἔριν καὶ χρεών.

81. ἡ δὲ τῶν ῥητόρων εἰσαγωγὴ πάντα τὰ θεωρήματα πρὸς τοῦτ' ἔχει τείνοντα καὶ κατὰ τὸν Ἡράκλειτον κοπίδων ἐστὶν ἀρχηγός.

82. πιθήκων ὁ κάλλιστος αἰσχρὸς ἀνθρώπων γένει συμβάλλειν.

83. ἀνθρώπων ὁ σοφώτατος πρὸς θεὸν πίθηκος φανεῖται καὶ σοφίαι καὶ κάλλει καὶ τοῖς ἄλλοις πᾶσιν.

80. (*Ibid.*, VI 28.)
One should see[77] that war is common[78] and justice is strife, and that everything is happening according to strife and necessity.[79]

81. (Philodemus, *Rhetorica* I, coll. 57, 62.)
([A possible reference to Pythagoras] Rhetoric is the prince of impostors.)[80]

82. (Plato, *Hippias major* 289a.)
(The most beautiful of apes is ugly when compared with the race of humans.)

83. (*Ibid.*, 289b.)
(The wisest person seems like an ape when compared with God; both in wisdom and beauty, and in all other things as well.)

---

[77] I follow Kirk in taking this as εἰδέναι, *contra* Kahn's εἰδέ[ναι]. The translation I have chosen suggests both understanding and visual perception, both of which are implicit in the etymology of the word. See **XVII**.

[78] I have put ἐόντα with πόλεμον (*contra* Kirk, Kahn, and others), making τὸν ξυνόν the grammatical subject of the phrase. In this way the middle placement of πόλεμον...ξυνὸν produces a more natural grammatical construction, while also emphasizing war's universal nature.

[79] I follow Diels and Kirk in reading *chreon* (χρεών), *contra* Kahn's questionable *chreomena* (χρεώμενα).

[80] Cf. fr. 129.

84. a) μεταβάλλον ἀναπαύεται.

b) κάματός ἐστι τοῖς αὐτοῖς μοχθεῖν καὶ ἄρχεσθαι.

85. θυμῶι μάχεσθαι χαλεπόν· ὃ γὰρ ἂν θέληι, ψυχῆς ὠνεῖται.

86. ἀπιστίηι διαφυγγάνει μὴ γιγνώσκεσθαι.

87. βλὰξ ἄνθρωπος ἐπὶ παντὶ λόγωι ἐπτοῆσθαι φιλεῖ.

88. ταὐτό τ' ἔνι ζῶν καὶ τεθνηκὸς καὶ [τὸ] ἐγρηγορὸς καὶ καθεῦδον καὶ νέον καὶ γηραιόν· τάδε γὰρ μεταπεσόντα ἐκεῖνά ἐστι κἀκεῖνα πάλιν μεταπεσόντα ταυτα.

84. (Plotinus, IV 8.1.)
   a) (It rests in changing.)[81]

   b) (It is distressing[82] to be weary with toil at the same tasks and always to be commencing.)[83]

85. (Plutarch, *Coriolanus* 22.2. [Cf. Aristotle, *Eudemian Ethics* II 7, 1223b 22.])
   It is hard to battle with one's own anger;[84] for whatever it wants it buys at the price of the soul.

86. (*Ibid.*, 38. [Cf. Clement, *Stromateis* V 88.4.])
   Disbelief[85] escapes recognition.

87. (Plutarch, *De audiendis poetis* 28d.)
   A stupid person tends to get aroused by every word.[86]

88. (*Ibid*. [Pseudo (?)], *Consolatio ad Apollonium* 106e.)
   The same is present[87]...living and dead, waking and sleeping, young and old. For these things having changed are those, and those things having changed are again these.

---

[81] This can also be read as an impersonal construction—'rest comes through change'.

[82] *kamatos* (κάματος) = toilsome, troublesome.

[83] I have translated *archesthai* (ἄρχεσθαι) as 'commencing', rather than employing the more popular translation (Diels, Burnet, Marcovich, etc.), 'to be ruled'. Additionally, I follow Bollack-Wismann in making τοῖς αὐτοῖς the object of μοχθεῖν; thus, the tasks are regarded as the causes of suffering, rather than those for whom one labors. This seems to me to be a more natural construction and lends itself more readily to the sense of the first part of the fragment.

[84] *thumoi* (θυμῶι) = heart, passion, desire, rage.

[85] *apistie* (ἀπιστίη)—Following Bollack-Wismann, I have translated this word in its nominative case, *contra* Diels, Freeman and Bywater, who treat it as a dative form.

[86] *panti logoi* (παντὶ λόγωι) = every conversation, every opinion, every consideration.

[87] Corrupt text.

89. τοῖς ἐγρηγορόσιν ἕνα καὶ κοινὸν κόσμον εἶναι, τῶν δὲ κοιμωμένων ἕκαστον εἰς ἴδιον ἀποστρέφεσθαι.

90. πυρός τε ἀνταμοιβὴ τὰ πάντα καὶ πῦρ ἁπάντων ὅκωσπερ χρυσοῦ χρήματα καὶ χρημάτων χρυσός.

91. ποταμῶι γὰρ οὐκ ἔστιν ἐμβῆναι δὶς τῶι αὐτῶι...οὐδὲ θνητῆς οὐσίας δὶς ἅψασθαι κατὰ ἕξιν <τῆς αὐτῆς>· ἀλλ' ὀξύτητι καὶ τάχει μεταβολῆς σκίδνησι καὶ πάλιν συνάγει (μᾶλλον δὲ οὐδὲ πάλιν οὐδ' ὕστερον, ἀλλ' ἅμα συνίσταται καὶ ἀπολείπει) καὶ πρόσεισι καὶ ἄπεισι.

92. Σίβυλλα δὲ μαινομένωι στόματι...ἀγέλαστα καὶ ἀκαλλώπιστα καὶ ἀμύριστα φθεγγομένη χιλίων ἐτῶν ἐξικνεῖται τῆι φωνῆι διὰ τὸν θεόν.

89. (Plutarch, *De superstitione* 166c.)
(For those awake there is one common world; but for those sleeping each deserts into a private world.)

90. (Plutarch, *De E apud Delphous* 388d-e.)
All things are compensation[88] for fire and fire for all things, just as goods are for gold and gold is for goods.

91. (*Ibid.*, 392b.)
(One cannot step twice into the same river...nor can one twice take hold of mortal substance in a stable condition; for by the quickness and swiftness of its alteration it scatters and gathers—at the same time it endures[89] and dissolves, approaches and departs.)

92. (Plutarch, *De Pythiae oraculis* 397a.)
(The Sibyl,[90] with raving mouth, utters[91] gloomy, unembellished and unperfumed things. Her voice reaches through a thousand years by means of the god.)

---

[88] *antamoibe* (ἀνταμοιβή) = payment, punishment, reward.

[89] *sunistatai* (συνίσταται) = combines, unites, continues.

[90] 'Sibyl' refers to a woman who, through the inspiration of a god (usually Apollo), made prophetic pronouncements about future events. The most ancient Sibyl was Herophile, who predicted the Trojan war.

[91] *phtheggomene* (φθεγγομένη) = speaks loud and clear.

93. ὁ ἄναξ, οὗ τὸ μαντεῖόν ἐστι τὸ ἐν Δελφοῖς, οὔτε λέγει οὔτε κρύπτει ἀλλὰ σημαίνει.

94. Ἥλιος γὰρ οὐχ ὑπερβήσεται μέτρα· εἰ δὲ μή, Ἐρινύες μιν Δίκης ἐπίκουροι ἐξευρήσουσιν.

95. ἀμαθίην γὰρ ἄμεινον κρύπτειν, ἔργον δὲ ἐν ἀνέσει καὶ παρ' οἶνον.

96. νέκυες γὰρ κοπρίων ἐκβλητότεροι.

97. κύνες γὰρ καταβαΰζουσιν ὧν ἂν μὴ γινώσκωσι.

93. (*Ibid.*, 404d.)
The lord[92] whose oracle is in Delphi neither declares nor conceals, but shows by a sign.[93]

94. (Plutarch, *De exilio* 604a.)
The sun will not surpass his measures; if he does the Furies,[94] ministers of justice, will find it out.[95]

95. (Plutarch, *Quaestiones conviviales* 644 f.)
(It is better to hide stupidity, but it is a hard task when relaxed and beside wine.)[96]

96. (*Ibid.*, IV 4.3. [Cf. Strabo, XVI 26.])
Corpses should be thrown out more than dung.

97. (Plutarch, *An seni respublica gerenda sit* 787c.)
Dogs bark at those they do not know.

---

[92] *anax* (ἄναξ)—a word used by Homer to refer to Apollo.

[93] The oracle of Delphi was the supreme religious authority in ancient Greece. Pythia, the priestess of Apollo, would enter an ecstatic trance and respond to questions put to her. These responses were then interpreted and put into verse by the priests of Apollo. According to legend, the Delphic oracle always spoke the truth. Yet, the truth was almost always stated in an obscure and ambiguous manner.

An example of this truth in ambiguity is found in Herodotus (I, 53 ff.). When Croesus, King of Lydia, consulted Pythia concerning his plan for making war against the Persian Empire, her response was that if he attacked the Persians, a great empire would fall. Overjoyed with this propitious prediction, Croesus went to war with Persia. As a result, a great empire fell; his own Lydian Empire.

[94] The Furies (Erinyes) are the children of Ouranos (Sky) and Gaia (Earth), who avenged blood-guilt and oath-breaking. See Hesiod, *Theogony*, 185, *Works and Days*, 803-04; and Aeschylus, *The Eumenides*.

[95] In light of the recently discovered 'Derveni Papyrus' (fr. A), some scholars have suggested that this fragment and fr. 3 are parts of a single passage in Heraclitus' published work.

[96] Cf. fr. 109.

98. αἱ ψυχαὶ ὀσμῶνται καθ' "Αιδην.

99. εἰ μὴ ἥλιος ἦν, ἕνεκα τῶν ἄλλων ἄστρων εὐφρόνη ἂν ἦν.

100. ...περιόδους· ὧν ὁ ἥλιος ἐπιστάτης ὢν καὶ σκοπὸς ὁρίζειν καὶ βραβεύειν καὶ ἀναδεικνύναι καὶ ἀναφαίνειν μεταβολὰς καὶ ὥρας αἳ πάντα φέρουσι....

101. ἐδιζησάμην ἐμεωυτόν.

a) ὀφθαλμοὶ γὰρ τῶν των ἀκριβέστεροι μάρτυρες.

102. τῶι μὲν θεῶι καλὰ πάντα καὶ ἀγαθὰ καὶ δίκαια, ἄνθρωποι δὲ ἃ μὲν ἄδικα ὑπειλήφασιν ἃ δὲ δίκαια.

98. (Plutarch, *De facie in orbe Lunae* 943e.)
(Souls smell things in Hades.)

99. (Plutarch [?], *Aqua an ignis utilior* 957a.)
(If there was no sun, it would be night.)[97]

100. (Plutarch, *Quaestiones Platonicae* 1007d-e.)
(The sun is commander and guardian of cycles; dividing, arbitrating, displaying, and bringing to light changes and seasons, which bring all things.)

101. (Plutarch, *Adversus Coloten* 1118c.)
I searched for myself.

   a) (Polybius, XIII 27.1.)
   (Eyes are more accurate witnesses than ears.)

102. (*Scholia Graeca in Homeri Iliadem*. H. Erbse, ed. I [1969], p. 445.
   [Cf. Porphyry, *Quaestiones Homericae*, Iliad IV 4.])
(For God all things are beautiful and good and just, but humans have supposed some things to be unjust, other things to be just.)

---

[97] *euphrone* (εὐφρόνη)—literally, 'the pleasant time'. See footnote 24.

103. ξυνὸν γὰρ ἀρχὴ καὶ πέρας ἐπὶ κύκλου περιφερείας.

a) συνιόντων τῶν μηνῶν ἡμέρας ἐξ ὅτου φαίνεται, προ—
τέρην νουμηνίην δευτέρην, ἄλλοτ' ἐλάσσονας μεταβάλλεται
ἄλλοτε πλεῦνας.

104. τίς γὰρ αὐτῶν νόος ἢ φρήν; δήμων ἀοιδοῖσι πείθονται
καὶ διδασκάλωι χρείωνται ὁμίλωι οὐκ εἰδότες ὅτι 'οἱ πολλοὶ
κακοί, ὀλίγοι δὲ ἀγαθοί'.

103. (Porphyry, *Quaestiones Homericae*, Iliad XIV 200.)
(Beginning and end are common in the circumference of a circle.)

a) (POXY 86 [1953] 3710, col. 2.34-47.)[98]
When the months converge,[99] from the moment it is revealed, it is changed; the days before and the days following the new moon are sometimes diminished, at other times increased.[100]

104. (Proclus, *In Alcibiades* I.)
What sense or wits[101] do they have? They are persuaded by the people's poets, the people serving as their teacher—not knowing that 'the many are worthless',[102] good people are few.

---

[98] This fragment is contained in the recently discovered 'Derveni Papyrus', and is therefore not included in Diels. My reason for placing it here is that is seems to make a point with respect to time that is similar to the point made in fr. 103 with respect to space. I would like to thank Professor David Sider and Rev. Joseph Koterski, SJ, for their help in translating and making sense of this very obscure fragment.

[99] The verb *sunionton* (συνιόντων) comes from the verb συνίημι, a word that Homer used to denote the coming together of hostile or antagonistic parties (*Iliad* I, 8; VII, 210).

[100] In the context of the fragment it is unclear what the two 'it's are referring to. In the interest of speculation I would suggest that they can be understood as referring to two different senses of the term *menon* (μηνῶν): μήν = month; and μηνάς = the moon. Thus, the 'it' that "is revealed" refers to the moon, while the 'it' that "is changed" refers to the month.
For the ancient Greeks the month began with the appearance of the new moon; when the new moon appeared, a new month began. Thus, the new moon represented a change from the last day of the old month to the first day of the new month (*noumenien*). The statement at the end of the fragment concerning the variable numbers of the days of the month has to do with the period of time between the appearance of one new moon and the next. This period, called a synodic month, is about 29.53 days. Owing to the half day (.53), the calendar month is sometimes 'diminished' to 29 days, and at other times it is 'increased' to 30 days.

[101] *phren*(φρήν) = mind, heart. This word is a cognate of *phronesis* (φρόνησις). See footnote 7. Also, cf. frs. 17, 112, 116.

[102] This is a saying attributed to Bias of Priene. Cf. fr. 39.

105. Ἡ. ἐντεῦθεν ἀστρολόγον φησὶ τὸν Ὅμηρον καὶ ἐν οἷς φησι 'μοῖραν δ' οὔ τινά φημι πεφυγμένον ἔμμεναι ἀνδρῶν' κτλ.

106. Ἡσιόδωι τὰς μὲν ἀγαθὰς ποιουμένωι, τὰς δὲ φαύλας, ὡς ἀγνοοῦντι φύσιν ἡμέρας ἁπάσης μίαν οὖσαν, ἑτέρωθι διηπόρηται. *unus dies par omni est.*

107. κακοὶ μάρτυρες ἀνθρώποισιν ὀφθαλμοὶ καὶ ὦτα βαρβάρους ψυχὰς ἐχόντων.

108. ὁκόσων λόγους ἤκουσα, οὐδεὶς ἀφικνεῖται ἐς τοῦτο, ὥστε γινώσκειν ὅτι σοφόν ἐστι πάντων κεχωρισμένον.

109. κρύπτειν ἀμαθίην κρέσσον ἢ ἐς τὸ μέσον φέρειν.

110. ἀνθρώποις γίνεσθαι ὁκόσα θέλουσιν οὐκ ἄμεινον.

111. νοῦσος ὑγιείην ἐποίησεν ἡδὺ καὶ ἀγαθόν, λιμὸς κόρον, κάματος ἀνάπαυσιν.

105. (*Scholia Homericae*, AT; Iliad XVIII 251.)
(Homer was an astronomer.)[103]

106. (Plutarch, *Camillus* 19.1.)
(Hesiod counted some days as good, others as bad, not knowing that the nature of every day is one.)[104]

107. (Sextus Empiricus, *Adversus mathematicos* VII 126.)
Eyes and ears are bad witnesses for people who have barbarian souls.

108. (Stobaeus, III 1.174.)
Of all accounts[105] I have heard no one has arrived at this: to discern that what is wise is separated from all things.

109. (*Ibid.*, III 1.175.)
It is better to hide stupidity or to bear moderation.[106]

110. (*Ibid.*, III 1.176.)
It is not better for people to obtain all that they want.

111. (*Ibid.*, III 1.177.)
Disease makes health sweet and good; hunger satiety, weariness repose.

---

[103] Cf. fr. 38 (and footnote 36), where the same claim is made about Thales.

[104] Cf. Hesiod, *Works and Days*, 765 ff.

[105] *logous* (λόγους) = words, rational discourses, reports.

[106] Cf. fr. 95.

112. σωφρονεῖν ἀρετὴ μεγίστη, καὶ σοφίη ἀληθέα λέγειν καὶ ποιεῖν κατὰ φύσιν ἐπαΐοντας.

113. ξυνόν ἐστι πᾶσι τὸ φρονέειν.

114. ξὺν νόωι λέγοντας ἰσχυρίζεσθαι χρὴ τῶι ξυνῶι πάντων, ὅκωσπερ νόμωι πόλις, καὶ πολὺ ἰσχυροτέρως. τρέφονται γὰρ πάντες οἱ ἀνθρώπειοι νόμοι ὑπὸ ἑνὸς τοῦ θείου· κρατεῖ γὰρ τοσοῦτον ὁκόσον ἐθέλει καὶ ἐξαρκεῖ πᾶσι καὶ περιγίνεται.

115. ψυχῆς ἐστι λόγος ἑαυτὸν αὔξων.

116. ἀνθρώποισι πᾶσι μέτεστι γινώσκειν ἑωυτοὺς καὶ σωφρονεῖν.

117. ἀνὴρ ὁκόταν μεθυσθῆι, ἄγεται ὑπὸ παιδὸς ἀνήβου σφαλλόμενος, οὐκ ἐπαΐων ὅκη βαίνει, ὑγρὴν τὴν ψυχὴν ἔχων.

118. αὐγὴ ξηρὴ ψυχὴ σοφωτάτη καὶ ἀρίστη αὔη ψυχὴ σοφωτάτη καὶ ἀρίστη.

112. (*Ibid.*, III 1.178.)

To be of sound mind[107] is the greatest excellence and wisdom; to speak and act with truth, detecting things according to their nature.[108]

113. (*Ibid.*, III 1.179.)

Thinking is common to all.

114. (*Ibid.*, III 1.179.)

Speaking wisely,[109] one should stoutly contend[110] for what is common to all, just as a city does for its law, but even more obstinately. For all human laws are nourished by the divine one; it prevails as it will and suffices for all and overcomes.[111]

115. (*Ibid.*, III 1.180a.)

The soul is a law that increases its own power.

116. (*Ibid.*, III 5.6.)

All people are able to know themselves and to learn self-control.[112]

117. (*Ibid.*, III 5.7.)

When a man gets drunk he is led by a beardless boy, staggering, unaware of where he walks—having a moist soul.

118. (*Ibid.*, III 5.8.)

A dry soul is sunlight, wisest and best.

---

[107] *sophronein* (σωφρονεῖν) = to be temperate, discreet, to show self-control. This is a cognate with *phronesis*.

[108] *phusin* (φύσιν) = natural qualities, constitution, condition.

[109] *xun nooi* (ξὺν νόωι)—literally, 'with mind', 'with purpose', 'with intent'.

[110] *ischurizesthai* (ἰσχυρίζεσθαι) = to put firm trust in, to persist obstinately.

[111] *periginetai* (περιγίνεται) = prevails, excels, is superior.

[112] *sophronein* (σωφρονεῖν)—cf. footnote 107.

119. ὡς ἦθος ἀνθρώπωι δαίμων.

120. ἠοῦς καὶ ἑσπέρας τέρματα ἡ ἄρκτος καὶ ἀντίον τῆς ἄρκτου οὖρος αἰθρίου Διός.

121. ἄξιον Ἐφεσίοις ἡβηδὸν ἀπάγξασθαι πᾶσι καὶ τοῖς ἀνήβοις τὴν πόλιν καταλιπεῖν, οἵτινες Ἑρμόδωρον ἄνδρα ἑωυτῶν ὀνήιστον ἐξέβαλον φάντες· ἡμέων μηδὲ εἷς ὀνήιστος ἔστω, εἰ δὲ μή, ἄλλη τε καὶ μετ' ἄλλων.

122. ἀγχιβατεῖν...ἀμφισβατεῖν· ἀγχιβασίην....

123. φύσις δὲ...κρύπτεσθαι φιλεῖ.

124. ...σάρμα εἰκῆ κεχυμένων ὁ κάλλιστος...[ὁ] κόσμος.

125. καὶ ὁ κυκεὼν διίσταται <μὴ> κινούμενος.

a) μὴ ἐπιλίποι ὑμᾶς πλοῦτος...' Εφέσιοι, ἵν' ἐξελέγχοισθε πονηρευόμενοι.

119. (*Ibid.*, IV 40.23. [Cf. Plutarch, *Quaestiones Platonicae* 999e.])
One's character is one's divine fortune.

120. (Strabo, I 1.6.)
The limit of dawn and evening[113] is the Bear;[114] and opposite the Bear is the Watchman[115] of luminous Zeus.

121. (*Ibid.*, XIV 25. [Cf. Diogenes Laertius, *Vitæ* IX 2.])
The Ephesians deserve, from the young men to the old, to be hanged, and to leave the city to the beardless youths, since they cast out Hermodorus, their best man, saying, 'let no one be the best among us: if he is, let him be so elsewhere and among others'.

122. (Suidas, *s.v.*)
([Word for 'Dispute'] stepping near.)

123. (Themistius, *Orationes* V 69b.)
Nature tends to hide itself.

124. (Theophrastus, *Metaphysica* 15.)
(The fairest order is a random pile of sweepings.)

125. (Theophrastus, *De vertigine* 9.)
(Even the potion[116] separates unless stirred.)

a) (Tzetzes, *Ad Aristoph. Plut.* 88.)
May wealth never fail you, people of Ephesus, in order that you may be convicted of your wickedness.

---

[113] *eous kai hesperas* (ἠοῦς καὶ ἑσπέρας)—also, 'east and west'.

[114] The constellation Ursa Major, which points to the north.

[115] This refers to the star Archturus. This southern star was used by the ancients to determine seasonal changes, and was referred to by the Greeks as 'the Bear-watcher'. See Aratus, *Phainomena*, 92. Also, cf. Marcovich, p. 338.

[116] *kukeon* (κυκεών)—a drink mentioned in the *Iliad* (XI 637 ff.), which was composed of wine, barley-meal, and grated cheese.

126. τὰ ψυχρὰ θέρεται, θερμὸν ψύχεται, ὑγρὸν αὐαίνεται, καρφαλέον νοτίζεται.

129. Πυθαγόρης Μνησάρχου ἱστορίην ἤσκησεν ἀνθρώπων μάλιστα πάντων καὶ ἐκλεξάμενος ταύτας τὰς συγγραφὰς ἐποιήσατο ἑαυτοῦ σοφίην, πολυμαθίην, κακοτεχνίην.

126. (Tzetzes, *Scholia ad exegesin in Iliadem*, p. 126.)
Cold things get warm; warm cools off; moist dries up; parched is wetted.

129. (Diogenes Laertius *Vitæ*, VIII 6.)
Pythagoras, son of Mnesarchus, practiced[117] inquiry more than all people, and choosing from these writings he made a wisdom of his own—much learning, fraudulent dealing.[118]

---

[117] *eskesen* (ἤσκησεν) = decorated, dressed up.
[118] *kakotechnie* (κακοτεχνίη)—This term implies craftiness with evil intent, a word probably coined by Heraclitus. Cf. fr. 81.
Although fr. 129 was considered by Diels to be a forgery, it is today generally accepted as authentic.

Analysis

Analysis of Themes

I UNITY

The primary motive of Heraclitus' metaphysics is the determination of structural unity in a world of apparent diversity and change. For Heraclitus, "unity is from everything and from everything is unity" (fr. 10). Wisdom (*sophie*; cf. **XI** [**A**]) consists in recognizing and attuning oneself to this unity (frs. 32, 33, 41, 50, 114). The unity theme underlies the majority of themes in Heraclitus.

(Note: fragments in parentheses indicate an implicit reference to the theme.)

Frs. 10, 32, 33, 41, 50, 57, 59, 60, 89, (91), 106, 114.

II LOGOS

The word λόγος (*logos*) is the earmark of Heraclitus' philosophy. He uses it to denote the underlying unity in the apparent diversity and change in the world. The word has a plethora of meanings, and Heraclitus often employs it to convey more than a single meaning. The etymological root of *logos* is ΛΕΓ (*LEG*), which suggests 'selecting', or 'picking out'. From this the word came to mean 'reckoning', as well as 'measure' and 'proportion'. Various other closely related meanings of *logos* are 'thought', 'reason', 'ground', as well as 'formula', 'law', and 'plan'. Utilizing some or all of these senses, Heraclitus employs the term to denote the universal order of the world (frs. 2, 50) as well as the mind's capacity to rationally discern this order—a capacity shared by everyone (fr. 113), but actualized only by those few individuals who possess wisdom (XI [A]).

Another important aspect of *logos* has to do with its connection to language. *Logos* shares a common etymological ancestry with the verb *lego* = to speak. *Logos* can therefore mean a spoken word, a statement, a discourse, an account, or a report (cf. **XVI**).

Bearing all of these meanings in mind, it appears that the purpose behind Heraclitus' adoption of the semantically rich *logos* is to emphasize that the structural order of the cosmos (**IX**), the rational order of the mind (**III**, **XIV**), and our linguistic ability to communicate our thoughts to others (**XVI**) all share a common feature. Each is an expression of the eternal *logos*.

Frs. 1, 2, 31b, 45, 50, 87, 108, 115.

III BEING COMMON

Heraclitus employs the terms ξυνός (*xunos*) and κοινός (*koinos*) to indicate commonalty (something shared by some things) and universality (something shared by all things). Thus, the beginning and the end of a circle are shared by some things, i.e., by every part of the circumference of the circle (fr. 103). According to Heraclitus, the systematic structure of the world (**IX**), the rational order of thought (**XIV**), and the meaningful structure of language whereby we convey our thoughts to others (**XVI**) must all have something in common which accounts for their mutual correspondences and systematic coordination. This something is the *logos* (**II**)—the universal order common to all things (frs. 2, 30), which is knowable by any rational being (frs. 113, 116).

Frs. 2, 30, 80, 89, 103, 113, 114.

IV FIRE

The image of fire is used by Heraclitus to symbolize the *logos* (**II**). Fire can be brought about through friction ('opposition' and 'strife'); for example, by rubbing two sticks together (**VII**). In the natural world fire represents change inasmuch as it radically alters the things upon which it feeds. Yet it also represents something unchangeable amid change. For while the shapes and the appearances of a fire are always changing, the fire retains its unity over time; for example, we ordinarily regard the fire lit in the fireplace early last evening as the same fire that died later that night (**VI**, **IX**).

In the human context fire is associated with the 'dry soul' of the enlightened individual, or the person who understands the fundamental order and process of the cosmos (XI [A], XIV).

Frs. 30, 31a, (43), (64), 65, 66, 67, 76, 90.

V GOD

Sometimes Heraclitus characterizes the structural unity of the world as 'God', 'Zeus', or 'the divine purpose'. In this sense 'God' is another name for *logos* (II)—the divine law upon which all gods, humans, and human laws depend (frs. 30, 114). 'God' and 'Zeus' are used both to metaphorically represent the cosmic order and, in the more traditional sense, to refer to the king of the Olympian pantheon (XV).

Frs. 32, (64), 67, 78, 83, 102, (114), (120).

VI CHANGE

It is only by understanding the nature of change that we are able to grasp the unity and rational order of the cosmos, or the *logos*. This theme emerges in two different contexts: (a) the changes occurring in the world (frs. 31a, 36, 67, 76, 88, 100, 125, 126); and (b) the changes characteristic of human experience—specifically, changes in perspective, changes in beliefs or attitudes, changes in values, and changes with regard to the names we apply to things (X) (frs. [8], [10], 12, 30, 36, 67, 84a, 91). According to Heraclitus, change occurs through the conflict and strife that arises when opposing forces interact (VII).

Frs. 6, 8, 10, 12, 30, 31a, 36, 67, (75), 76, 84a, 88, 91, 100, (125), 126.

VII OPPOSITION AND STRIFE

For Heraclitus, change (VI) is a universal process generated through opposition (*antixoos*) and strife (*eris*). By understanding the essential interdependence and harmony of things in opposition, we may come to recognize the hidden harmony and underlying unity of these things (fr. 8) (VIII). Heraclitus discusses opposition and strife in at least three different contexts: (a) opposition as the fundamental cosmic process (frs. 8, 10, 51) (IV); (b) the conceptual oppositions and interdependencies among our ideas, whereby one idea is said to depend upon its 'opposite' (frs. 23, 51, 57, 60, 67, 88, 91, 99, 103, 111, 126) (X); and (c) opposition as war or battle (frs. 24, 53, 67, 80, 85).

The following fragments contain references to specific oppositions used by Heraclitus to illustrate (a), (b), and (c).

Frs. 10, (53), 59, 60, 62, 65, 67, (71), (84a), 88, 91, 103, 111, 120, 126.

VIII HARMONY

In addition to the idea of a concordance of sounds, the word ἁρμονία (*harmonia*) also conveys the idea of things being fastened and joined together for a purpose. Thus, Homer and Herodotus employ the term to describe the joining together of a ship's planks.

Heraclitus insists that the most beautiful harmony comes from things in conflict (fr. 8) or at variance (fr. 51) with one another (VII). This is a hidden harmony, superior to any perceivable concordance (fr. 54). It is discernible only by the person with wisdom (XI [A]); that is, one who understands the lawful order and systematic connectedness that underlies the apparent diversity and disjointedness of appearances.

Frs. 8, 51, 54.

IX ORDER, JUSTICE, AND THE SUN

The term κόσμος (*kosmos*) denotes an order or arrangement, and is used by Heraclitus to refer to the structural integrity of the world. This order was created neither by gods nor by human beings, for both are equally subject to it (fr. 30). It is the divine purpose which "steers all things" in a lawful and rational manner (frs. 41, 71). Heraclitus uses the metaphorical image of fire to represent this cosmic principle of unity in change (IV). The cosmos is the "fire ever-living," burning and being extinguished in eternal, measured cycles (frs. 30, 65). Fire is also suggested in the image of the thunderbolt, which guides and manages the world (fr. 64). This brings to mind Zeus, the personification of the eternal cosmic order (V), who used thunderbolts to control his enemies. This idea of cosmic fire is furthermore implicit in Heraclitus' references to the sun. The movements and cycles of the sun express order and regularity (fr. 94), and serve to order and regulate the lawful cycles of nature (fr. 100).

Heraclitus also refers to the cosmic order with the name Justice (Δίκη, *Dike*). In Greek mythology Dike was the daughter of Zeus (the personification of power) and Themis (the personification of law). For Heraclitus, Justice represents the divine order that underlies the regularities in natural and human laws (frs. 94, 114). Justice bestows retribution upon whatever attempts to transgress these laws (frs. 28b, 94), and is identified with strife (*eris*)—that according to which everything happens (frs. 80, 8) (**VII**).

In fragment 124, Theophrastus quotes Heraclitus as saying, "the fairest order is a random pile of sweepings." At first blush, this remark seems completely paradoxical. For the cosmos is said to be a necessary and eternal order—a closed system that is knowable by the rational mind. And we ordinarily regard the idea of a necessarily determined and rationally knowable system as being antithetical to the idea of a system subject to the operations of chance and randomness.

What Heraclitus seems to be suggesting here is that these seemingly antithetical notions are, like many others he discusses, actually just two sides of the same coin. (See, for example, the way up/the way down [fr. 60]; day/night, winter/summer, war/peace, satiety/hunger [fr. 67]; life/death, waking/sleeping [fr. 88].) In other words, both the apparent regularities and the apparent irregularities with regard to the laws of nature are expressions of a higher, more pervasive law that ultimately governs both. From the limited perspective of the ordinary person (**X**, **XI** [**B**]), the cosmos might appear to be lawful at one time, and unlawful, or random, at another time. From this point of view, however, one is "thoroughly beguiled regarding the knowledge of manifest things" (fr. 56). The person possessing wisdom, on the other hand, is not deceived by the appearances (**XI** [**A**]). Such a person is able to know things "according to their nature" (fr. 112), and to understand the single purpose which underlies and directs both the apparent orders and the apparent disorders in nature (fr. 41). Thus, while to the ordinary person "nature tends to hide itself" in the appearances (fr. 123), the person with wisdom recognizes the 'hidden harmony' expressed in apparent randomness—an order that is superior to the merely apparent order (fr. 54). See **VIII** and **XVIII**.

Order—frs. 1, (23), 30, 41, 64, 80, 90, 100, 124.
Justice—frs. 23, 28b, 80, 94.
The Sun—frs. 3, 6, (16), 94, 99, 100.

X RELATIVITY

The Relativity theme indicates that no particular human perspective, no specific human value or belief, and no name we apply to a thing is as fixed and stable as we may perceive, conceive, or believe it to be. Each is subject to change and is utterly dependent upon its 'opposite'. Typically, Heraclitus makes this point by way of an apparent paradox. Here I will characterize two important and closely related variations on this theme.

(A) *The Limitations of Human Perspectives and the Relativity of Values*

According to Heraclitus, most people live as though they possess a private purpose (fr. 2). Ordinary people mistakenly treat the personal world of opinions and beliefs as the real world (fr. 89), and make judgments about things purely on the basis of such subjective and limited perspectives. Thus, they may regard gold as valuable and garbage as worthless; or clean water as healthy and sea water as unhealthy. Yet from the perspective of a donkey, garbage is more valuable than gold (fr. 9); and for a fish, sea water is drinkable and life-preserving (fr. 61). Similarly, pigs prefer muck and mire to clean water (frs. 13b, 37), and chickens bathe in dust (fr. 37). So the same thing can be both good and bad, valuable and worthless, depending upon one's perspective.

The same point is made by comparing the limited perspective of the individual to the unlimited perspective of God (V), or *logos*: "for God all things are beautiful and good and just, but humans have supposed some things to be unjust, other things to be just" (fr. 102). Furthermore, the person who regards himself as wise and another as childish may himself be regarded as childish by God (fr. 79); and even the wisest person "seems like an ape when compared with God; both in wisdom and beauty, and in all other things as well" (fr. 83).

In addition to the relativity of attitudes between animals, humans, and God, Heraclitus points out that one's own particular perspective changes radically as circumstances and contexts change. Thus, in the visible world I depend upon sight as my most reliable source of information (frs. 55, 101a). However, if everything turned into smoke, I would depend upon the sense of smell (fr. 7). And in the lightless region of Hades, souls rely upon the sense of smell rather than upon sight (fr. 98).

Heraclitus insists that whatever attitude we have at any given time is ultimately dependent upon what we regard as its opposite. In other words, without disease and sickness, we would not regard health as good; and the pleasures we find in having enough to eat and in resting would mean nothing unless we have known the displeasures of hunger and weariness (fr. 111).

In calling attention to the great variety of individual perspectives upon the world, their inter-relationships, interdependencies, and the tendency of each to change, Heraclitus is suggesting that all such perspectives share a common dependence upon the *logos*—the underlying unity and 'higher harmony' implicit in this diversity. Wisdom involves overcoming the particularity and restriction of one's own limited perspectives (**XI [A]**) and recognizing the universality expressed in all such attitudes. In other words, the wise person is one who recognizes that all of the diverse perspectives are the perspectives of a self-identical rational soul—a subjective expression of the *logos*, which underlies and unifies these various perspectives through time. (Concerning the relationship between the individual soul and the *logos*, see **XIV**.)

Frs. 7, 58, 62, 72, 79, 82, 83, 88, 102, 111, 124.

(B) *The Changeableness of Things and the Relativity of our Beliefs about Them*

From the ordinary human point of view, the world contains a variety of things that we regard as stable and essentially unchanging. While I am looking at the tree in the yard, it appears as something fixed and substantial, as something that remains the same through time. Thus, I believe that the tree I am seeing now is the same tree I saw a moment ago, the same tree I saw three weeks ago, etc. And I apply the same name or description ('this tree in the yard') to it at different times.

According to Heraclitus, all of the things that appear to be stable and more or less permanent are actually undergoing continual change and alteration (**VI**). At one level this is obvious to anyone who has observed that cold things become warm, wet things become dry, etc. (fr. 126). But Heraclitus is doing much more than calling attention to the changeableness of a thing's accidental properties (its color, temperature, smell, etc.). He insists that the thing's substantiality, or its stability and endurance through time, is mere appearance: one cannot "twice take hold of mortal substance in a stable condition; but by the quickness and swiftness of its alteration it scatters and gathers—at the same time it endures and dissolves, approaches and departs" (fr. 91). In several places Heraclitus uses the image of a river or stream to suggest that what we ordinarily regard as something stable and enduring is actually fleeting and ever-changing; thus, one cannot step into the same river twice (frs. 12, 49a, 91).

It is a basic tenet of Heraclitus' philosophy that things which appear to be fixed and stable are really mutable and ever-changing; and that the person who lacks understanding fails to recognize the fundamental vicissitude underlying the apparent stability of things. On the other side of the coin, such a person also fails to recognize the fundamental unity and integrity underlying things which he or she regards as distinct from, or even opposed to, one another (XI). Thus, while those who lack wisdom may distinguish between the way up the hill and the way down the hill on the basis of their relative and limited perspectives (that is, in terms of whether they are at the bottom or at the top of the hill), those with wisdom recognize that "the way up and down is one and the same" (fr. 60). Similarly, while most people draw a radical distinction between being alive and being dead, being awake and being asleep, being young and being old, etc., the person with wisdom recognizes that each of these notions is intimately connected with its apparent contrary, and that "the same is present" in both (frs. 88, 62).

Frs. 12, 49a, 60, 62, 88, 91, 103, 124, 126.

XI WISDOM AND IGNORANCE

(A) *Wisdom*

For Heraclitus, the person with wisdom (σοφίη, *sophie*) understands the underlying, unitary structure of the *logos* and recognizes that "all is one" (fr. 50), despite the apparent diversity of particular things and particular perspectives (fr. 108) (X). The wise person is not one who has learned many different things (fr. 40), but rather one who has inquired into many things (frs. 35, 55) and has come to know the order which is common to all of them (frs. 2, 30) (III, VIII, IX). Such a person does not "randomly reckon" concerning the nature of things (fr. 47), but rather rationally understands and obeys the underlying plan and purpose of the universal order (frs. 32, 33, 41, 50) (XII).

Heraclitus describes the wise person as one who is awake. For this individual sees the world we all share in common, while sleeping (i.e., ignorant) people see only the limited and private worlds of their dreams (XII). Also, the wise person is said to possess a 'dry soul'; that is, a soul which is identified with the universal fire, or the *logos* (fr. 118) (II, IV, XIV). According to Heraclitus, people who possess wisdom are extremely rare and valuable (frs. [22], 104, 112, 118, [49], 69) (XIII [A]).

Frs. 32, 35, 41, 50, 83, 108, 112, 118.

(B) *Ignorance*

Since "nature tends to hide itself" (fr. 123), the vast majority of people are ignorant of the rational structure of the world. Such people fail to see beyond their own limited, individual perspectives (X), and have no notion of the underlying unity and harmony of the cosmic order. They know only their own private purposes (fr. 2); they only believe in their own limited opinions (frs. 17, 70); and they shut themselves off from the universal *logos*. They know "neither how to listen nor how to speak" (fr. 19), and are compared to deaf people (fr. 34) or those who are asleep (frs. 1, 73, 89) (**XVI, XII**). They become suspicious and negatively aroused by new ideas (frs. 87, 97), and seek to isolate themselves in their ill-founded and changeable opinions (frs. 70). Such people fail to utilize their capacity for rational discernment and are described as having barbarian souls (fr. 107). Like dumb cattle, they are mostly concerned with satisfying their appetites (frs. [4], 29), and they are easily persuaded through self-interest (fr. 11).

In contrast to the dry soul associated with the wise individual, the ignorant person has a moist soul. Heraclitus says that "it is delight or death for souls to become moist" (fr. 77). With respect to the soul's delight, he compares the ignorant person to someone who is drunk. It is difficult for drunk people to hide their ignorance and stupidity (fr. 95). Like the drunk, the man with a moist soul is easily led, "staggering, unaware of where he walks" (fr. 117), and he forgets where he is going (fr. 71). His view of reality is distorted, he is easily persuaded by appearances and ill-formed opinions, and he lacks self-control (**XIII [B]**). Heraclitus suggests that after physical death the moist soul of the ignorant person becomes water and is absorbed in the endless cycles of organic nature (**XIV**).

Frs. 1, 2, 17, (19), 34, 40, 51, 70, 87, (89), 95, 97, 109, 117.

XII WAKING / SLEEPING

Heraclitus uses the distinction between waking and sleeping as a metaphor for the states of wisdom and ignorance, respectively. The person who is awake is aware of a systematic world which everyone shares in common (**III, IX, XI [A]**), whereas the sleeping person is in a private world (frs. 89, 21) (**X, XI [B]**). Heraclitus insists that "it is necessary to follow the common," (fr. 2), and that "we should not act or speak like sleeping people" (fr. 73).

Frs. 1, 21, 26, 73, 75, 88, 89.

XIII GOOD PEOPLE / BAD PEOPLE

(A) *Good People*

Heraclitus' social views were those of a profound aristocrat. Persons of value are few while the majority of people are worthless (fr. 104) and are compared to a herd of sheep (fr. 29). A good person is worth ten thousand ordinary people (fr. 49), and the most noble person seeks a greater destiny and greater reward than do less noble people (fr. 25). The noble person strives for "ever-flowing glory among mortals" (fr. 29). In the fragments Heraclitus mentions two good and noble men: Bias of Priene and Hermadorus of Ephesus (see Index of Persons).

Goodness is generally described as a quality that accompanies wisdom (**XI** [A]); and a good action is one which is consistent with the 'divine purpose' (**V**).

Frs. 13a, (22), (25), 28, 29, 39, 49, 104, (108), 121.

(B) *Bad People*

Heraclitus' sharp criticism of the majority of people does not rest upon the usual aristocratic distinction of good or bad in terms of birth. He suggests that goodness accompanies wisdom; and wisdom, insofar as it involves rational thought, is available to everyone (fr. 113). Thus knowledge and self-control—the characteristics of a good person—can be achieved by anyone (fr. 116). The ignorance of bad people is something that they bring upon themselves by allowing themselves to be beguiled by appearances (frs. 56, 72), and by turning a deaf ear to the cosmic harmony of the *logos*. Such people do not know "how to listen" (fr. 19) (**XVI**). Their knowledge is checked by their limited personal perspectives (**X**), and their ignorance is reinforced through their acceptance of popular opinions, such as those expounded by the poets Homer, Hesiod, and Archilochus (see Index of Persons). Bad people are compared to sated sheep and cattle, who blindly follow the path of least resistance (frs. 29, 11).

Heraclitus points to his own people, the Ephesians, as an example of bad people. He chastises them for their stupidity, greed and wickedness, and suggests that every male citizen past puberty should be hanged (frs. 121, 125).

Frs. 1, 2, (11), 14, (15), 17, 19, (22), 29, 34, 44, 56, 57, (70), (72), (78), 87, (102), 104, (106), 113, 116, 121, 125a.

XIV LIFE, DEATH, AND THE SOUL

To the ordinary person, life and death appear to be two distinct and mutually exclusive states. For Heraclitus, however, they represent mutually dependent aspects of a single process (frs. 15, 48). All change in nature occurs as a continuous cycle of life and death (frs. 20, 36, 88).

While Heraclitus indicates that we cannot imagine what happens to us after death (fr. 27), he nevertheless suggests some interesting ideas concerning physical death and the nature of the soul. The soul is regarded as the seat of rational thought. It is the subjective expression of the *logos*—the same *logos* expressed objectively in the cosmic structure and processes of the world (II, III, VI, IX). Wisdom involves the recognition of this sameness (III, XI [A]). In this way the soul "increases its own power" (fr. 115) and thereby becomes a dry soul. It is dry to the extent that it is identified with the universal fire (fr. 118) (IV). He suggests that when a wise person dies, the soul is united with this fire (*logos*) (fr. 26), and so achieves a kind of immortality. On the other hand, when an ignorant person dies, that person's moist soul dies as well (fr. 77). It is transformed into water, then into earth (fr. 36), and is incorporated into organic nature in much the same way as the physical body.

Life / Death—frs. 15, 20, 21, 26, 27, 36, 48, 52, 62, 63, 77, 88.
The Soul—frs. 36, 45, 77, 85, 98, 107, 115, 117, 118.

XV GODS AND RELIGION

In the fragments Heraclitus refers to several traditional Greek divinities: Justice (*Dike*), the Sun (*Helios*) the Furies (*Erinyes*), Zeus, Hades, Dionysos, and Apollo. The word 'justice' is generally used to designate the quality rather than the goddess, while the word 'sun' is usually employed to denote the object rather than the god (IX). In fragment 94 the Furies, the primeval 'ministers of justice' who avenge blood-guilt, are described as overseers of the regular activities of the sun (which is itself the 'commander and guardian' of the natural cycles and changes in the world [fr. 100]). Zeus is sometimes depicted as 'the wise one', or the personification of the *logos* (V) (frs. 32, [64]), while at other times he is cast in his more traditional role (fr. 120). Hades and Dionysos are mentioned in fragment 15, where they appear to be metaphorical images of death and life, respectively. Apollo, the god of reason and of prophesy, is enigmatically referred to in fragments 92 and 93.

Heraclitus characterizes the *logos* (or 'war', i.e., the active processes of strife and opposition [VII]) as "the father of all, the king of all, [who] has shown some as gods, others as humans; [who] has made some slaves, others free" (fr. 53). This, along with what he says in fragment 62, suggests that both humans and gods share a common origin in, and dependence upon, the *logos*. The order of the world is the same for gods and human beings; yet, it is independent of both (fr. 30). He goes on to describe the traditional gods as intermediaries between the *logos* and humans. They are superior to humans (fr. 79); yet, like us, they are dependent upon the *logos*. This suggests a hierarchy with the *logos* at the top, the traditional gods in the middle, and human beings below. And in light of what he says elsewhere, this hierarchy may extend below adult human beings to include children (fr. 79) and apes (frs. 82, 83).

Heraclitus is extremely critical of the popular religious practices of his day. The ancient Greek custom of staining oneself with blood to atone for blood-guilt is compared to a person's washing with dirt—an activity that is both irrational and ineffectual. The devotee's praying to an object of worship is compared to someone's talking to a house; for both houses and religious objects are mere inanimate things (fr. 5). Furthermore, the public religious rites in honor of Dionysos are said to be utterly corrupt and shameless (frs. 14, 15) inasmuch as they serve to reinforce the common ignorance and misunderstanding of the true nature of God, or *logos* (V). According to Heraclitus, "Dionysos and Hades are one and the same" (fr. 15). The idea here seems to be that the traditional polytheistic religions tend to regard the divine nature in terms of different and distinct gods, in much the same way that the ignorant person particularizes and individuates things (and his or her perspectives upon things) in the world. In either case people fail to recognize the essential commonalty and interdependence of those things which they believe to be separate and distinct.

Despite the fact that Heraclitus calls the rites surrounding the worship of Dionysos 'shameless' and 'unholy', he suggests that, for the participants, such rites might serve as 'remedies' (*akea*) (fr. 68). Dionysos was the god associated with vegetation, fertility, sexuality, and ecstasy, and he was represented in the public festivals with phallic images. It has been suggested that, in calling the perceptions of these 'shameless' things 'remedies', Heraclitus is pointing out the cathartic psychological effects such perceptions have upon the worshipers—effects comparable to those of tragic theater upon the audience. (See footnote 69.)

Gods—frs. 5, 24, 30, 32, 53, 62, 67, (78), 79, 83, 92, 102, (114).
Religion—frs. 5, 14, 15, 68, 69.

XVI LISTENING

Listening is naturally associated with the *logos* in the sense of a spoken word, statement, account, report, or discourse (II). Heraclitus 'expounds' (the word *epeon* was used by the Greeks to describe oracular pronouncements) the *logos*, and the listener may respond in one of two ways. Most listeners will hear only the particular words and phrases, and will not grasp the general underlying meanings expressed in the account (*logos*) (fr. 1). Like deaf people (fr. 34), they do not know how to listen (fr. 19). They possess barbarian souls, and their ears are bad witnesses with regard to the truth (fr. 107) (XI [B]). Such people lack understanding both before and after they hear the true account of things (fr. 1).

On the other hand, a few listeners will hear and understand the underlying meaning of Heraclitus' account—the *logos*. These are the people whose comprehension goes beyond the mere words, beyond the particular things, to an understanding of the universal and rational structure of the world. They listen, not to Heraclitus' words, "but rather to the *logos*," and thus they recognize "that all things are one" (fr. 50) (XI [A]).

Frs. 1, 2, 19, 34, 50, (55).

XVII SEEING

In English there is a close relationship between the cognitive verbs 'to see' and 'to understand'. We say things like, 'I see what you mean', and we use words such as 'insight' and 'clarity' with reference to understanding. Similarly the perfect tense of the Greek verb εἴδω (*eido* = to see) is οἶδα (*oida*), which literally means 'I have seen', but which was used to mean 'I know'.

As in the case of listening (XVI), Heraclitus uses the notion of seeing in two different ways. On the one hand, most people see only the appearances of particular things and are thoroughly beguiled by them (frs. 46, 56) (X, XI [B]). Here the eyes serve as bad witnesses of the truth (fr. 107). On the other hand, some people are able to disregard popular opinions and conjectures, and to see for themselves, through rational inquiry, the true nature of reality (frs. 55, 101, 101a). In this way they are able to gain insight into the hidden structural integrity of the world, and to see the whole that is "superior to the visible" parts (fr. 54) (VIII, XI [A]).

Frs. 21, 46, (54), 55, 56, 101a, 107.

XVIII A CHILD

Heraclitus employs the metaphorical image of a child to represent randomness and chance. At one level a child represents simple arbitrariness. In this sense human opinions are children's playthings (fr. 70). Such opinions are formed and maintained on the basis of one's limited personal perspectives rather than on one's rational understanding of the universal *logos*. Thus, they are subject to change and modification (X). The ignorant person, the person with a moist soul, is like the drunk being led by a "beardless boy, staggering, unaware of where he walks" (fr. 117). This person's actions are dictated by opinions, and these opinions are based upon the deceptive and beguiling appearances. The arbitrariness here is in stark contrast to the rational understanding and self-control exhibited by the person who recognizes and 'obeys' the universal order of the *logos*.

The image of a child is also used to indicate a state of innocence. In this sense the young child represents one who is not beguiled by appearances, and who has not yet been tainted and restricted by popular opinions (fr. 121). The person with wisdom, then, resembles a child (XI [A]). One particularly enigmatic expression of this wisdom-in-innocence idea is contained in fragment 52: "Life is a child playing, moving the pieces in a game: kingship belongs to the child." Here we have the suggestion of apparent order (a game with various pieces that are moved according to certain rules), and apparent disorder or randomness (a child who may not know the rules, or who may choose to ignore them and make up new rules).

The strange and paradoxical character of fragment 52 closely resembles the enigmatic and obscure pronouncement in fragment 124: "the fairest order is a random pile of sweepings" (see IX). While Heraclitus repeatedly characterizes the *logos* as the thoroughly rational and purposive order of the cosmos, in frs. 52 and 124 he indicates that this order is further expressed in the appearance of randomness, in the seeming arbitrariness of a child's whim and in a pile of sweepings.

I believe that the point of these paradoxical statements is basically to admonish us not to draw a false dichotomy between the apparent order and regularity of nature, and the apparent irregularities and operations of chance which we sometimes encounter. Both the apparent regularities and the apparent exceptions are actually expressions of a deeper, more pervasive, order—an order not expressible in terms of either, taken in isolation. Thus, in fragment 52, the game (its pieces and its rules) represents the way nature ordinarily appears to us; that is, as a systematic structure governed by specific rules. However, given our limited understanding of the true nature of reality, we sometimes encounter things that we are unable to fully understand—things which seem to be incomprehensible in terms of the rules that govern the apparent order of nature, and which appear to be as arbitrary and irrational as a child's whim. Yet, everything is actually subject to a single law, the *logos*, which is itself subject to no laws or limitations.

Therefore, "kingship belongs to the child" inasmuch as the child may freely and spontaneously make, break, and change the rules of play. From the adult point of view, such alterations appear as arbitrary inconsistencies with no reason or purpose. But for the child each change of the rules expresses a higher purpose—the purpose of play, or the innocent activity of free creation. Like the primary motivating principle underlying the cosmos, the primary motivating principle underlying a child's playing a game is hidden in what appears to be disjointed and fragmented activities. Yet each is a case of self-determined, creative activity.

Frs. 20, 52, 70, 74, (79), (117), (121).

Index of Persons

Archilochus of Paros

Archilochus, a poet who lived around the beginning of the seventh century BC, was famous for his iambic poetry, elegies, hymns and lampoons. He was said to have been responsible for various metrical inventions used by later Greek poets.

Fr. 42.

Bias of Priene

Bias, son of Teutames, lived around 550 BC. Very little is known about him, despite the fact that he was one of the Seven Sages of the ancient world. Heraclitus attributes to him the saying, "the many are worthless."

Frs. 39, 104.

Hecataeus of Miletus

Hecataeus was a popular writer who lived around 550 BC. He was best known for his geographical works, his genealogies of the great mythological families, and his records of the local fables that he encountered during his extensive travels.

Fr. 40.

Hermodorus of Ephesus

Hermodorus was probably a contemporary of Heraclitus. Apart from Heraclitus' reference, there is no mention of Hermodorus among ancient Greek writers. However, a later legend (perhaps based on Heraclitus' reference) made Hermodorus a co-author of the Twelve Tablets—the first codification of Roman law.

Fr. 121.

Hesiod

Hesiod was a Boeotian poet who probably lived a short time after Homer (perhaps the late eighth century BC). He was the author of two important works: *Theogony* (an extremely influential mythological account of the origins of the gods and of the world); and *Works and Days* (a practical handbook for successful living). Hesiod's influence upon the ancient Greeks was second only to Homer's.

Frs. 40, 57, 106.

Homer

Homer was the most famous and influential of all Greek poets. His *Iliad* and *Odyssey* were for the ancient Greeks the primary sources of historical, moral, and literary education. He probably lived around the early to middle eighth century BC.

Frs. 42, 56, 105.

Pythagoras of Samos

Pythagoras (fl. c. 532 BC) was an early Greek philosopher whose main themes were the mathematical structure of the cosmos and the transmigration of the soul. He is accredited with having started a mystery school that flourished throughout the classical period. While the doctrines of Pythagoras had a tremendous effect upon the development of Plato's mature philosophy, Heraclitus appears to have regarded Pythagoras as a charlatan.

Frs. 40, (81), 129.

Thales of Miletus

Thales lived in the early sixth century BC, and is regarded as the first philosopher and physicist. According to Thales, water is the basic substance, or *archê*, of the world. He was also an astronomer of great renown, and is credited with having predicted the solar eclipse of 585 BC.

Fr. 38.

Xenophanes of Colophon

Xenophanes was a philosopher and poet who lived around the mid-sixth century BC. He is best known for his strong criticisms of the traditional Greek religious views concerning the immortality of the soul and the nature of the gods. He was also concerned with pointing out the limitations of human knowledge.

Fr. 40.

Index of Terms

A accord, sung together (v.) = (συνᾴδω)—10

 account (n.) = (λόγος)—1, 2, 31b, 39, 45, 50, 108, 115

 actions (n.) = (ἔργον)—1

 active (adj.) = (ἐγερτί)—63

 agree (v.) = (ὁμολογέω)—50, 51; (συμφέρω)—8, 10

 air (n.) = (ἀέρ, ἀήρ)—76

 all things, everything, all people (n.) = (πᾶσ / πᾶσα / πᾶν)—1, 7, 8, 10, 30, 41, 50, 53, 64, 66, 80, 90, 100, 102, 108, 113, 114, 129

 always (adv.) = (ἦν ἀεί)—30

 ape (n.) = (πίθηκος)—82, 83

 appear, seem (v.) = (δοκοίη)—5; (φαίνω)—72, 83

 apprehending, laying hold of (part.) = (σύλληψις)—10

 approach (v.) = (πρόσειμι)—91

 assertion (n.) = (λόγος)—1, 2, 31b, 39, 45, 50, 108, 115

 associate (v.) = (ὁμιλέω)—72

attempt (v.) = (πειράω)—1

awake (adj.) = (ἐγερθέντες)—1, 21, 26, 88, 89

B Bacchants (n.) (worshippers of Dionysos) = (Βάκχοις)—14

bad (adj.) = (κακός)—104, 107

beardless youth (n.) = (ἄνηβος)—117, 121

beauty (prefix) = (καλλι-)—8, 82, 83, 102, 124

become (v.) = (γίνομαι)—1, 8, 20, 31b, 36, 56, 63, 75, 77, 80, 110

beguile (v.) = (ἐξαπατάω)—56

being (n.) = (ἐόντος from εἰμί)—1, 2, 7, 80

believe (v.) = (δοκέω)—17, 27, 28

best (adj.) = (ἀρίστη)—118

best, most noble person (n.) = (ἄριστος)—29, 49

birth (n.) = (γένεσις)—76, 77

bring to light (v.) = (ἀναφαίνω)—100

bow (n.) = (τόξον)—48, 51

C caste out (v.) = (ἐκβάλλω)—42, 121; (ἐκβλητότεροι)—96

cattle (n.) = (L. *boves*)—4

change (v.) = (ἀλλοιόω)—67; (μεταβάλλεται)—103a

character (n.) = (ἦθος)—78, 119

child (n.) = (παῖς)—20, 52, 56, 70, 74, 79, 117

choose (v.) = (αἱρέω)—9, 29

Index of Terms

cold (adj.) = (ψυχρός)—126

combine (v.) = (συμφέρω)—8, 10

come into being (v.) = (γίνομαι)—1, 8, 20, 31b, 36, 56, 63, 75, 77, 80, 110

common, universal (adj.) = (κοινός)—2, 89; (ξυνός)—2, 80, 103, 113, 114

compensation (n.) = (ἀνταμοιβή)—90

concordance of sounds (n.) = (ἁρμονία)—8, 51, 54

conflagration, flaring fire (n.) = (πυρκαϊή)—43

contest (n.) = (ἀγών)—42

continuous (adj.) = (διηνεκής)—72

corpse (n.) = (νέκυς)—96

cosmos (n.) = (κόσμος)—30, 75, 89, 124

crooked, twisted (adj.) = (σκολιός)—59

D day (n.) = (ἡμέρα)—57, 67, 72, 103a, 106

dead (n., v.) = (τέθνηκα; ἀποθνῄσκω)—26, 62, 88

dead body (n.) = (νεκρός)—63

deaf (adj.) = (κωφός)—34

death (n.) = (ἀποθάνατος)—27; (θάνατος)—14, 21, 36, 48, 62, 76, 77

deceive (v.) = (ἐξαπατάω)—56

delight, pleasure (n.) = (ἡδονή)—13b, 67; (τέρψις)—77

depart (v.) = (ἄπεις; ἀφείς)—91

depart from, leave behind (v.) = (ἀπολείπω)—56, 91

deserving (adj.) = (ἄξιος)—42

destiny, fate (n.) = (μόρος)—20, 25

differ, be at variance (v.) = (διαφέρω)—8, 10, 51, 72

different (adj.) = (ἕτερος)—12

Dionysos (n.) (god associated with fertility, wine, and ecstasy) = (Διονύσιος)—15

disbelief (n.) = (ἀπιστίη)—86

discern, distinguish (v.) = (διαγνώσκω)—7

discourse (n.) = (λόγος)—1, 2, 31b, 39, 45, 50, 108, 115

disease (n.) = (νόσος)—58, 111

dispense, dissolve (v.) = (διαχέω)—31b

display (v.) = (ἀναδείκνυμι)—100

dissonant, sung apart (adj.) = (διᾷδος)—10

distinct (adj.) = (διηνεκής)—72

distinguish, divide into parts (v.) = (γινώσκω)—5, 17, 28, 57, 86, 97, 108, 116; (κρίνω)—66; (διαιρέω)—1

divide (v.) = (ὁρίζω)—100

divine (adj.) = (θεῖος)—78, 114

do, create, act (v.) = (ποιέω)—1, 5, 15, 30, 73, 106, 111, 112

donkey (n.) = (ὄνος)—9

down (adv.) = (κάτω)—60

dry (v.) = (αὐαίνω)—126

Index of Terms

dry, parched (adj.) = (καρφαλέος)—126

E   ears (n.) = (ὤντων, from οὖς)—101a

earth (n.) = (γῆ)—31a, 31b, 36

end, limit (n.) = (πέρας)—45, 103

escape (v.) = (διαφυγγάνω)—86

esteem (n.) = (λόγος)—1, 2, 31b, 39, 45, 50, 108, 115

eternal (adj.) = (ἀεί)—1, 6, 30

ever-flowing (adj.) = (ἀέναος)—29

ever-living (adj.) = (ἀείζωον)—30

excellence (n.) = (ἀρετή)—112

existing things (n.) = (ἐόντα)—7

extinguish, put out (v.) = (ἀποσβέννυμι)—26, 30

eyes (n.) = (ὀφθαλμός)—26, 101a, 107

F   father (n.) = (πατήρ)—53

few (adj.) = (ὀλίγος)—104

fight, battle (v.) = (μάχομαι)—44, 85

find out (v.) = (ἐξεύρημα)—94

fire (n.) = (πῦρ)—30, 31a, 65, 66, 76, 90

flow (v.) = (ἐπιρρέω)—12

foot (n.) = (πούς)—3

forget (v.) = (ἐπιλανθάνομαι)—1, 71

fortune (n.) = (δαίμων)—79, 119

free (adj.) = (ἐλεύθερος)—53

Furies (n.) (primordial daughters of Ouranos [Sky] and Gaia [Earth], who avenge blood-guilt; they are often depicted as winged women with serpents twined in their hair) = (' Ερινύες)—94

G gather together (v.) = (συνάγω)—91

gentleman (n.) = (χαρίεντα)—13a

god (n.) = (δαίμων)—79, 119

God (n.) = (θεός)—5, 24, 30, 53, 67, 83, 92, 102

gold (n.) = (χρύσεος)—9, 22, 90,

good (adj.) = (ἀγαθός)—102, 106, 111

good people (n.) = (ἀγαθοί)—104

grasped (v.) = (ἅπτεται)—26, 30, 91

grasping, seizing (part.) = (κατάληψις)—28, 66

ground (n.) = (λόγος)—1, 2, 31b, 39, 45, 50, 108, 115

guardian, watcher (n.) = (φυλακός)—63

H Hades (n.) (god who ruled the underworld, or the underworld itself) = (Ἀΐδης)—15, 98

happen (v.) = (γίνομαι)—1, 8, 20, 31b, 36, 56, 63, 75, 77, 80, 110

harmony (n.) = (ἁρμονία)—8, 51, 54

health (n.) = (ὑγιείνα)—111

hear, listen (v.) = (ἀκούω)—1, 19, 34, 50, 79, 108

Index of Terms

hearing (part.) = (ἀκοή)—55

heat, warm up (v.) = (θέρω)—126

herds, flocks (n.) = (κτήνεα)—29

hide, conceal (v.) = (κρύπτω)—93, 95, 109, 123

honor (v.) = (τιμάω)—24; (προτιμάω)—55

hope (n.) = (ἔλπις)—18, 27

human (adj.) = (ἀνθρώπειος)—3, 78, 114; (ἀνθπώτινος)—70

hunger (n.) = (λιμός)—67, 111

I   ignorant (adj.) = (ἄπειρος)—1

imagine (v.) = (δοκέω)—17, 27, 28

immortal (adj.) = (ἀθάνατος)—62

increase (v.) = (αὔξησις)—115

inquiry (n.) = (ἱστορίη)—35, 129

inscrutable (adj.) = (ἀνεξερεύνητον)—18

insight (n.) = (γνώμη)—41

insolence, violence (n.) = (ὕβρις)—43

intention (n.) = (γνώμα)—78

invisible, hidden (adj.) = (ἀφανής)—54

itself, its own (reflex. pron.) = (ἑωυτῶι)—51, 115, 116

J   joined (v.) = (ἅπτεται)—26, 30, 91

joy (n.) = (ἄθυρμα)—70

just (adj.) = (δίκαια)—102

Justice (n.) = (Δίκη, δίκη)—23, 28b, 80, 94

K king (n.) = (βασιλεύς)—53

kingship (n.) = (βασιληίη)—52

know (v.) = (γινώσκω)—5, 17, 28, 57, 86, 97, 108, 116; (εἴδω)—56, 57, 80, 104; (ἐπίσταμαι)—19, 41, 57

knowledge (n.) = (γνῶσις)—56

L lack understanding (v.) = (ἀξύνετοι)—1, 34

law (n.) = (λόγος)—1, 2, 31b, 39, 45, 50, 108, 115; (νομός)—33, 44, 114

learning (part.) = (μάθησις)—55

leave behind (v.) = (καταλείπω)—20

lie, deceit (n.) = (ψευδής)—28, 46

life (n.) = (αἰών)—52; (βίος)—48, 62

light (n.) = (φάος)—26

lighted (v.) = (ἅπτεται)—26, 30, 91

lightning-storm (n.) = (πρηστήρ)—31a

limit, boundary (n.) = (τέρμα)—120

live (v.) = (ζώω)—2, 20, 26, 62, 63, 88

Lord (n.) (Apollo, god of light, reason, harmony, and prophesy) = (ἄναξ)—93

lover of wisdom (n.) = (φιλοσόφος)—35

Index of Terms

M mad, raving, insane (adj.) = (μαίνομαι)—5, 15, 92

make cold (v.) = (ψύχω)—126

make wet (v.) = (νοτίζω)—126

man (n.) = (ἀνήρ)—35, 117

man, mankind, person (n.) = (ἄνθπωτος)—1, 5, 14, 24, 26, 27, 30, 53, 56, 61, 69, 82, 83, 87, 102, 107, 110, 116, 119

mind, heart (n.) = (φρήν)—104

mingle (v.) = (συμμίσγω)—67

moist (adj.) = (ὑγρός)—77, 117, 126

months (n.) = (μηνῶν)—103a

mortal (adj.) = (θνητός)—62

most people, many people (n.) = (οἱ πολλοί)—2, 17, 29, 104

much learning (n.) = (πολυμαθίη)—40, 129

must (implying a sense of duty or obligation) (v.) = (χρή; cf. δεῖ = necessary)—35, 43, 44, 80, 114

N name (n.) = (ὄνομα)—32, 48; (v.) = (ὀνομάζω)—67

nature (n.) = (φύσις)—1, 112, 123

necessary (adj.) = (δεῖ; cf. χρή = must)—2, 13a, 73, 74

necessity (n.) = (χρέων)—80

need, want (n.) = (χρησμοσύνη)—65

new, young (adj.) = (νέος)—6, 88

night (n.) = (εὐφρόνη)—26, 57

not knowing (v.) = (ἀγνοέω)—106

not (negation) (adv.) = (μή). This modifier can be found in the following phrases:

    escapes recognition = (μὴ γινώσκεσθαι)—86
    if these things didn't exist = (μὴ ἦν εἰ ταῦτα)—23
    let no one be the best = (μηδὲ εἷς ὀνήιστος ἔστω)—121
    (the fee) they receive is not worthy = (μηδὲν ἄξιον... λαμβάνειν)—58
    they don't know = (μὴ γινώσκωσι)—97
    unobserved = (μὴ δυνόν)—16
    we shouldn't (randomly reckon) = (μή συμβαλλώμεθα)—47

= (οὐ, οὐδείς, οὐκ, οὔτε, οὐχί). This modifier can be found in the following phrases:

    being unaware = (οὐκ ἐπαΐων)—117
    does not teach = (οὐ διδάσκει)—40
    he failed to recognize = (οὐκ ἐγίνωσκεν)—57
    he will not find = (οὐκ ἐξευρήσει)—18
    it has no purpose = (οὐκ ἔχει γνώμας)—78
    it is not better = (οὐκ ἄμεινον)—110
    neither declares nor conceals = (οὔτε λέγει οὔτε κρύπτει)—93
    no one has arrived = (οὐδείς ἀφικνεῖται)—108
    nor do they understand = (οὐδὲ...γινώσκουσιν)—17
    not knowing = (οὐ τι γινώσκω)—5
    not knowing = (οὐκ εἰδότες)—104
    not knowing how to listen or how to speak =(οὐκ ἐπιστάμενοι οὐδ' εἰπεῖν)—19
    not listening = (οὐκ ἀκούσαντας)—50
    unwilling and willing = (οὐκ ἐθέλει καὶ ἐθέλει)—32
    one cannot step... nor (take hold) of mortal substance = (οὐκ...ἐμβῆναι...οὐδὲ θνητῆς οὐσίας)—91
    should neither act nor speak = (οὐ...ποιεῖν καὶ λέγειν)—74
    they don't anticipate or imagine = (οὐκ ἔλπονται οὐδὲ δοκέουσι)—27
    they don't comprehend = (οὐ φρονέουσι)—17
    they don't understand = (οὐ ξυνιᾶσιν)—51
    they would not know = (οὐκ ἂν ᾔδεσαν)—23
    (was made) neither by the gods nor humans = (οὔτε τις θεῶν οὔτε ἀνθρώπων)—30

(what) we neither saw nor seized = (οὔτε εἴδομεν οὔτ' ἐλάβομεν)—56
whole and not whole = (οὐχ ὅλα, [ὅλα καί])—10
will not surpass = (οὐχ ὑπερβήσεται)—94
you will not discover = (οὐκ ἐξεύροιο)—45

O obey (v.) = (πείθω)—33

observe (v.) = (ἐπιφράζω)—5

old (adj.) = (γηραιός)—88

one (adj.) = (εἷς)—49

one (n.) = (μία)—59, 60, 106

one, unity (n., adj.) = (ἕν)—10, 32, 33, 41, 50, 51, 89, 114

opinion (n.) = (δόξασμα)—70

opposition (n.) = (ἀντίξοος)—8

oracular statement (n.) = (ἐπέων)—1, 2

order (n.) = (κόσμος)—30, 75, 89, 124

origin (n.) = (γένεσις)—76, 77

other people (n.) = (τῶν ἄλλων)—39

overstep, transgress, surpass (v.) = (ὑπερβαίνω)—94

P peace (n.) = (εἰρήνη)—67

people (n.) = (δῆμος)—44, 104

perceive (v.) = (γινώσκω)—5, 17, 28, 57, 86, 97, 108, 116

period or cycle of time (n.) = (περίδος)—100

pigs (n.) = (ὕες)—13b

plan (n.) = (γνώμη)—41

play (v.) = (παίζω)—52

plaything (n.) = (ἄθυρμα)—70

pleasure (n.) = (ἡδονή)—13b, 67

polluted, defiled (adj.) = (μιαρός)—61

private, personal (adj.) = (ἴδιος)—2, 89

proportion (n.) = (λόγος)—1, 2, 31b, 39, 45, 50, 108, 115

pure (adj.) = (καθαρός)—61

purified (adj.) = (ἀποκεκαθαρός)—69

purpose, intention (n.) = (γνώμα)—78; (γνώμη)—41; (φρόνησις)—2

Q quench (v.) = (σβέννυμι)—43

R randomly (adv.) = (εἰκῆ)—47

reason (n.) = (λόγος)—1, 2, 31b, 39, 45, 50, 108, 115

reckon, compare (v.) = (συμβάλλω)—47, 82

recognition (n.) = (γνῶσις)—56

remedies (n.) = (ἀκέα)—68

remember (v.) = (μιμνήσκω)—71

report (n.) = (λόγος)—1, 2, 31b, 39, 45, 50, 108, 115

rest (v.) = (ἀναπαύω)—20, 84a, 111

reward, share (n.) = (μοίρα)—25

river, stream (n.) = (πόταμος)—12, 49a, 91

rule, be strong (v.) = (κρατέω)—114

S   sacrifice (n.) = (θυσία)—69

same (adj.) = (αὐτοῖσι)—12; (τὸν αὐτόν)—30, 31b

satiety, surfeit (n.) = (κόρος)—29, 65, 67, 111

scatter (v.) = (σκίδνημι)—91

sea (n.) = (θάλασσα)—31a, 31b, 61

see (v.) = (εἴδω)—56, 57, 80, 104; (ὁράω)—21, 46

self-conceit (n.) = (οἴησις)—46

sentinel, watcher (n.) = (σκοπός)—100

separate, set apart (v.) = (διΐστημι)—125

separately (adv.) = (κεχωρισμένως, from χωρίζω)—108

serve (v.) = (χραόμαι)—104

show, indicate (v.) = (φράζω)—1, 103a

Sibyl (n.) (prophetic spokeswoman of Apollo) = (Σίβυλλα)—92

sight (n.) = (ὄψις)—55

slain in battle (n.) = (ἀρηΐφατος)—24

slave (n.) = (δοῦλος)—53

sleep (v.) = (εὕδω)—1, 21, 26; (καθεύδω)—73, 75, 88

sleep (n.) = (ὕπνος)—21

smell (v.) = (ὀσμάομαι)—98

soul (n.) = (ψυχή)—36, 45, 77, 85, 98, 107, 115, 117, 118

sound mind, self-control (v.) = (σωφρονέω)—112, 116

speak (v.) = (λέγω)—32, 73, 93, 112, 114; (εἶπον)—19

spirit (n.) = (δαίμων)—79, 119

stain, defile (v.) = (μιαίνω)—5

statement (n.) = (λόγος)—1, 2, 31b, 39, 45, 50, 108, 115

steer (v.) = (οἰακίζω)—64

steering (part.) = (ἐκυβέρνησις)—41

step (v.) = (ἐμβαίνω)—49a, 91

stir, move (v.) = (κινέω)—125

straight (adj.) = (εὐθεῖα)—59

strange (adj.) = (ξένα)—72

strife (n.) = (ἔρις)—8, 81

stupidity (n.) = (ἀμαθίη)—95, 109

stupid person (n.) = (βλάξ)—87

suffice (v.) = (ἐξαρκέω)—114

summer (n.) = (θέρος)—67

sun (n.) = (ἥλιος)—3, 6, 94, 99, 100

sunlight (n.) = (αὐγή)—118

sweet (adj.) = (ἡδύς)—111

T ten thousand (adj.) = (μυριάς)—49

think (v.) = (φρονέω)—17, 113

thunderbolt (n.) = (κεραυνός)—64

truth (n.) = (ἀληθέα)—112

turn back upon itself (v.) = (παλίντροπος)—51

turning, reversal (n.) = (τρόπος)—31a

U ugly (adj.) = (αἰσχρός)—82

understand (v.) = (ἐπίσταμαι)—19, 41, 57; (φρονέω)—17, 113

understanding, mind, good sense (n.) = (νόος)—40, 104, 114

unite, combine (v.) = (συνίστημι)—91

unjust (adj.) = (ἄδικα)—102

unobserved, escape notice (v.) = (λανθάνω)—1, 16

up (adv.) = (ἄνω)—59, 60

V visible, manifest (adj.) = (φανερός)—54, 56

W wakeful (adj.) = (ἐγερτί)—63

walk, step (v.) = (βαίνω)—117

war (n.) = (πόλεμος)—53, 67, 80

warm (adj.) = (θερμός)—126

water (n.) = (ὕδωρ)—12, 13b, 36, 61, 76

way (n.) = (ὁδός)—45, 59, 60, 71

weariness (n.) = (κάματος)—84b, 111

whole (adj.) = (ὅλα)—10

will (n.) = (γνώμα)—78; (φρόνησις)—2

will be (ἔσται, from ἔστι)—30

winter (n.) = (χειμών)—67

wisdom (n.) = (σοφίη)—83, 112, 129

wise (adj.) = (σοφός)—32, 41, 50, 108

wisely (adv.) = (ξὺν νόωι)—114

wiser (adj.) = (σοφώτερος)—56

wisest (adj.) = (σοφώτατος)—85, 118

word (n.) = (λόγος)—1, 2, 31b, 39, 45, 50, 87, 108, 115

words (n.) = (ἐπέων)—1, 2

world-order (n.) = (κόσμος)—30, 75, 89, 124

worthless, base (adj.) = (κακός)—104, 107

Z Zeus (n.) (king of the Olympian gods) = (Ζηνός)—32; (Διός)—120

Bibliography

Aeschylus. *Aeschyli Tragoediae*. Edited by D. Page. London: Oxford University Press, 1975.

Autenrieth, G. *A Homeric Dictionary*. Translated by R.P. Keep. Norman: University of Oklahoma Press, 1972.

Bollack, J. and H. Wismann. *Héraclite ou la séparation*. Paris, 1972.

Burkert, W. "Eraclito nel Papiro di Derveni: due nuove testimoniaze," *Atti del Symposium Heracliteum 1981*. Edited by L. Rosetti. Rome: 1983, 1.37-42.

Burnet, J. *Early Greek Philosophy*. New York: Meridian Books, 1958.

Buttmann, P.K. *Lexilogus, or A Critical Examination of the Meaning and Etymology of Numerous Greek Words and Passages, Intended Principally for Homer and Hesiod*. Third edition. Translated by J.R. Fishlake. London: John Murray, 1846.

Bywater, I. *Heracliti Ephesii Reliquiae*. Chicago: Argonaut, Inc., 1969.

Cleve, F.M. *The Giants of Pre-Sophistic Greek Philosophy*. The Hague: Martinus Nijhoff, 1965.

Denniston, J.D. *The Greek Particles*. Second edition. Oxford: University Press, 1970.

Diels, H. *Herakleitos von Ephesos*. Berlin: Weidmannsche Buchhandlung, 1901.
—*Die Fragmente der Vorsokratiker*. Edited by W. Kranz. Vol. I. Berlin: Weidmannsche Buchhandlung, 1934.

Diogenes Laertius. *Vitae philosophorum*. Edited by H.S. Long. Oxford: University Press, 1964.

Fränkel, H. "A Thought Pattern in Heraclitus," *American Journal of Philosophy* 59 (1938): 309-37.

Freeman, K. *Ancilla to the Pre-Socratic Philosophers*. Cambridge: Harvard University Press, 1978.
—*The Pre-Socratic Philosophers: A Companion to Diels, 'Fragmente der Vorsokratiker'*. Oxford: Basil Blackwell, 1953.

Gigon, O. *Untersuchungen zu Heraklit*. Leipzig, 1935.

Goodwin, W.W *A Greek Grammar*. London: St. Martin's Press, 1977.

Guthrie, W.K.C. *The Greeks and Their Gods*. Boston: Beacon Press, 1955.
—*A History of Greek Philosophy*. Volume II. London: Cambridge University Press, 1965.
—*The Greek Philosophers*. New York: Harper Colophon Books, 1975.

Harvey, P. *The Oxford Companion to Classical Literature*. Oxford: University Press, 1937.

Herodotus. *Herodoti historiae*. Edited by C. Hude. Oxford: University Press, 1912.

Hesiod. *Hesiodus carmina*. Edited by A. Rzach. Stuttgart: B.G. Teuber Verlag., 1958.

Hölscher, U. "Paradox, Simile, and Gnomic Utterance in Heraclitus," reprinted in *The Pre-Socratics: A Collection of Critical Essays*. Edited by A.P.D. Mourelatos. Garden City: Anchor Books, 1974.

Homer. *Iliad*. Edited by D.B. Monroe. Oxford: Clarendon Press, 1958, 1960.
—*The Odyssey*. Edited by A.T. Murray. Cambridge: Loeb Classical Library, 1946, 1953.

Hussey, E. *The Pre-Socratics*. New York: Charles Scribner's Sons, 1972.

Jaeger, W. *Paideia*. Third edition. Translated by G. Highet. Oxford: University Press, 1946.

Kahn, C.H. "On Early Greek Astronomy," *The Journal of Hellenic Studies* 90 (1970): 99-116.
—*The Art and Thought of Heraclitus*. Cambridge: University Press, 1979.

Kirk, G.S. "The Michigan Alcidamas-Papyrus; 'Heraclitus Fr. 56D, The Riddle of the Lice'," *Classical Quarterly* 44 (1950): 149 ff.
—"Natural Change in Heraclitus," *Mind* 60 (1951): 35-42.
—*Heraclitus: The Cosmic Fragments*. Cambridge: University Press, 1962.
—with Raven, J.E. and M. Schofield. *The Presocratic Philosophers*. Second edition. Cambridge: University Press, 1983.

Liddell, H.G. and Scott. *An Intermediate Greek-English Lexicon*. Seventh edition. Oxford: University Press, 1889.

Lloyd, G.E.R. *Magic, Reason and Experience*. Cambridge: University Press, 1979.

Marcovich, M. *Heraclitus: The Greek Text with a Short Commentary*. Merida: Los Andes University Press, 1967.

Marinone, N. and F. Guala. *Complete Handbook of Greek Verbs*. Milan: Casa Editrice Principato, 1969.

Nilsson, M.P. *Griechische Feste*. Leipzig, 1906.

Owen, W.B. and E.J. Goodspeed. *Homeric Vocabularies*. Norman: University of Oklahoma Press, 1975.

Owens, J. *A History of Ancient Western Philosophy*. New York: Appleton, Century and Crofts, Inc., 1959.

Patrick, G.T.W. *The Fragments of the Work of Heraclitus of Ephesus: on Nature*. Baltimore: N. Murray, 1889.

Pharr, C. *Homeric Greek*. Norman: University of Oklahoma Press, 1966

Reinhardt, K. *Parmenides und die Geschichte der griechischen Philosophie*. Bonn, 1916.
—*Vermächtnis der Antike. Gesammelte Essays zur Philosophie und Geschichtsschreibung*. Edited by C. Becker. Göttingen, 1966.

Sider, D. "Heraclitus B 3 and 94 in the Derveni Papyrus," *Zeitschrift für Papyrologie und Epigraphik* 69 (1987): 225-28.

Sinclair, T.A. *A History of Classical Greek Literature: from Homer to Aristotle*. New York: Collier Books, 1962.

Snell, B. "Die Sprache Heraklits," *Hermes* 61 (1926): 353-81.
—*Heraklit Fragmente; griechisch und deutsch*. Tübingen: E. Heimeran, 1965.

Stöhr, A. *Heraclit*. Vienna, 1920.

Vlastos, G. "On Heraclitus," *American Journal of Philology* 76 (1955): 337-68

West, M.L. *Early Greek Philosophy and the Orient*. Oxford: University Press, 1971.

Zeller, E. *Outlines of the History of Greek Philosophy*. Thirteenth edition. New York: Dover Books, 1931.